CENTRAL
FLORIDA
THOROUGHBREDS

CENTRAL FLORIDA
THOROUGHBREDS

A History of Horses in the Heart of Florida

CHARLENE R. JOHNSON

Charleston · London

THE
History
PRESS

Published by The History Press
Charleston, SC 29403
www.historypress.net

Copyright © 2014 by Charlene R. Johnson
All rights reserved

First published 2014

Manufactured in the United States

ISBN 978.1.62619.075.7

Library of Congress CIP data applied for.

To Dick Chazal, who made the first book, Florida Thoroughbred, *possible.*

CONTENTS

FOREWORD

This is the truly remarkable story of the founding of the "Horse Capital of the World,"™ in Ocala, Florida. From starting slowly in the 1930s to making huge strides in the 1950s and exploding in the '70s and '80s, the "Sport of Kings" became a huge part of Marion County, Florida, and the Thoroughbred industry nationwide.

This is not just a story of the growth of an industry. It is a testament to what can be accomplished with the dream, drive and determination of a few individuals working together for a common goal. Many people contributed along the way, but without question, the founding fathers of yesteryear played a huge role in the industry as we know it today.

My attorney, Lanny Curry, sent me a congratulatory note recently for Ocala Stud being named the 2013 TOBA National Breeder of the Year. He wrote, "Papa Joe would be proud of you and your sons for that outstanding honor—or he might say he did all the hard work and y'all are just reaping the benefits." I think no truer words were ever written.

The individuals have changed, farm names have changed, the business has changed and the cast of characters may not be as colorful as it once was, but the industry is alive and well. That is because, as John Nerud said years ago, "Ocala is the best place in the world to breed, raise and train a horse."

He's right.

—MICHAEL O'FARRELL

Acknowledgements

B oth my dedication and my thanks go to those who supported this book with their contribution of collateral, time and energy.

Jim Jernigan has been a photographer of Marion County's evolution since 1947. Although he has photographed everything that has gone on in the county, his special support of the early Thoroughbred pioneers, at a time when no one else thought they warranted taking such pictures, brings that history to life. He still goes to work every day at his studio in Ocala, where his children carry on his artistic tradition. I am very grateful for his enthusiastic support of this project.

Angie Draper painted the first equine heroes of Florida's budding industry in 1968, and she continued to do so into the 1990s. Educated at the Ringling School of Art and Design, she was also the illustrator for several entries in Walter Farley's *Black Stallion* series of children's books, and she was commissioned to paint the top racehorses in Panama and Mexico. Her work has been featured in the National Museum of Racing in Saratoga Springs and has appeared in many equine magazines. Angie's life was dedicated to horses, as well as to the support of the Black Stallion Literacy Project. I feel very privileged that she also supported this book, elevating it to such esteemed company.

The words of Chuck Tilley, captured in some fifteen scrapbooks, though almost never dated or the publication noted, nonetheless provided many delightful details. His regular columns in the *Daily Racing Form*, *Morning Telegraph* and, of course, *The Florida Horse* magazine provide a history not found

ACKNOWLEDGEMENTS

anywhere else. He and Karl Koontz, the magazine's first editor, are together responsible for getting the earliest words out to a doubting public about the authenticity of a new industry exploding in unprecedented numbers and with unprecedented speed, much like the horses they chronicled.

Lastly, Tammy Gantt of the Florida Thoroughbred Breeders' and Owners' Association (FTBOA) interrupted her own work numerous times to answer questions, dig into closets and trust her personal library to me; this book could not have been written without her help. And, of course, to the many people who were willing to talk to me and dig out their own pictures and memories, I say, "Thank you!"

INTRODUCTION

In 2005, the American Horse Council conducted a survey that, at last, told the truth of it. The Department of Agriculture census verified that truth: Marion County in central Florida has more horses and ponies than any other single county in the United States. This patch of "sand, alligators and palm trees," as long-ago Kentuckians used to scoff, has more than proven itself as an important breeding and training ground for every imaginable breed of equine, from miniature horses that could have been used in *The Hobbit* movie series to impossibly long-maned and long-tailed Gypsy Vanner horses straight out of a little girl's dream come true.

The county is also host to one of the largest horse shows in the country. HITS, or Horses in the Sun, generates between $6 and $7 million in the two months it is held in the county. The new Florida Horse Park hosts many eventing, dressage and driving competitions, and the county is part of the 110-mile Greenways corridor sweeping across the state and allowing riders long, safe trail rides. More than nine hundred farms provide homes to these horses and ponies, including some of the finest racehorses in the world.

It is the Thoroughbred that is the topic of this tale, the instigator of all this popularity among the horsey set. Central Florida is second in the United States for the highest concentration of Thoroughbreds, on a par with only three other places in the world: Lexington, Kentucky; Newmarket, England; and Chantilly, France. The State of Florida hosts about 600 Thoroughbred farms and training centers, of which 75 percent, some 430, are located in Marion County. More than seventy thousand acres of this lovely, rolling green countryside are devoted to the Thoroughbred industry alone.

Known as the "Horse Capital of the World,"™ Ocala/Marion County in 2013 was home to about 35,300 Thoroughbreds. This high concentration is strongly supported by a network of services such as veterinarians, feed and tack retailers, blacksmiths, equine dentists and horse transportation companies. According to the American Horse Council Economic Impact Study of 2005, the industry creates an economic impact of more than $2.2 billion annually and provides twenty-seven thousand full-time jobs, more than thirteen thousand in the Ocala/Marion County area. This is a higher number than the entire population of the county at the time the industry began in the 1930s.

These Thoroughbred farms and training centers have produced forty-seven National Champions, six Kentucky Derby winners, seven Preakness Stakes winners, six Belmont Stakes winners, twenty-four Breeders' Cup Champions and six Horses of the Year. The crowning glory is one Triple Crown winner. Only eleven horses have ever won that Classic series—the Derby, Preakness and Belmont—but none has succeeded since 1978, when one bred and trained in the Sunshine State claimed that coveted crown.

Besides home-breds, however, many Thoroughbreds bred in other states are also raised, trained, wintered over and in other ways benefit from what Florida has to offer: year-round warmth and sunshine.

For many years, the Thoroughbred industry has been one of the most important industries in Florida, on a par with tourism and citrus. But in its formative years, the struggle was uphill. Out-of-state horsemen accustomed to the tame, rolling green of Newmarket or Lexington, with their neat white fences, could not imagine raising blue-blooded racehorses in the wilds of 1930s–1950s Florida, a land more reminiscent of the Wild West. No one involved in the Thoroughbred industry elsewhere took the visionary Floridians seriously.

The story of the unprecedented growth of a multibillion-dollar industry is as good as any cowboy and Indian movie. Against all odds and scoffers, riding the economic surf of the 1980s and 2000s, the tale continues to be rife with heroism, passion and faith. It is a tale of dedication, persistence and an absolute belief in a land that much of the North American population considered as strange as a foreign country. It is a story rich in characters both equine and human, and it continues to be the stuff of which dreams and riches are made.

When it comes to racehorses, the animal follows the dollar; it is, after all, a business based on gambling. But it is also a sport, if the "Sport of Kings." The farms on "Million Dollar Row" or the one patterned after the television series *Dallas*, as well as the view of copper steeples set against green, richly fertilized, rolling pastures, certainly attest to the fact that some of the wealthiest people in the world own, breed and raise racehorses. But so do some of the poorest. Today's industry sees a much different face from the times when old money traveled from New York via train and plane to Hialeah and Cuba to enjoy the tropics, gambling and fast horses. A vast majority of today's horsemen and horsewomen are just like you and me: ordinary people with a dream and a passion for the most noble animal on earth. "My kingdom for a horse" is easily understood by such people.

Without the horse, the tale of Marion County and central Florida would be a very different story. The land itself is a fairy tale come true, the ultimate rags-to-riches story. And so we begin, once upon a time…

Chapter 1

IT'S IN THE WATER

In 1976, veteran turf writer Chuck Tilley wrote:

Climate, soil and water are assets. A limestone ridge runs through Central Florida, curves north and westward to the panhandle section and into Georgia. The limestone mined in Florida is softer than that found further north and can be crushed into near powder form. Topography is an advantage. The gentle sloping hills with a minimum of outcropping of rocks allows young horses to run and play from their foaling date throughout their training period. Giant live oaks that grew side by side in uncleared hammock land that never had fertilization other than nature's, provide shade in hot weather. Gulf and ocean breezes compromise the semi-tropical heat. There is more than 50 inches of annual rainfall…Florida horse farmers took what nature provided them; then went to work.

On July 21, 1984, Marion County's local paper, the *Ocala Star Banner*, reported that a six-inch-long skull fossil was found in a freshly cut phosphate mine. Scientists knew that this tiny, three-toed horse existed due to the many teeth and other bone bits found around the state of Florida, but never before had a whole skull been found. This horse, called *Nannipus minor*, "dwarf horse," lived between 2 and 15 million years ago.

"Bone Valley" in nearby Polk County, where most of the phosphate mines exist, is so named for being one of the richest fossil deposits in the world for ancient horses. Florida is often cited as one of the most likely places to find equine fossils. Certainly, many local farmers, equine and otherwise, can discuss the bones and teeth found while excavating for a new barn or a training track. It seems clear: First Horse loved Florida.

Why not? He was doubtless a migratory animal, journeying to warmer climes to avoid the worst of the cold weather and then heading back north when it got too warm. Even Fredrico Tesio, one of the greatest horsemen of all time, competed his horses in Italy or the southern coast of France during the colder winter months and then returned north in the spring.

By the time of European contact, though, horses were gone from the American continents. It was not until Spanish explorers began bringing horses (along with pigs, guns and diseases), first to the Caribbean islands and then to Florida, that the escaping equines, having found paradise on earth, bred and spread north and west until they changed the face of the American continent and American history forever. Speedier transportation and beasts of burden instantly changed every native culture that survived the first one hundred years of post-contact annihilation. Nothing would ever be the same again. Evolution usually requires thousands of years to effect a significant change, but the introduction of the horse to indigenous people changed the look, the feel, the very soul of the Americas nearly overnight.

In later years, the horse would again change the face of Florida with equal speed. When farmers and racing aficionados first conceived of the idea of breeding a great racehorse in Florida in the 1930s, horsemen in other equine centers laughed—mostly Kentuckians, since horsemen in Newmarket and Chantilly still found it astounding that *any* place in the upstart colonies could raise a great racehorse. But to blue-blooded horsemen, Florida, with its ocean, sand and sinkholes, really did seem like a foreign land unfit for the production of the hot-blooded and sometimes delicate equine racing form.

What it takes to grow good bone in any livestock, be it cattle or horses, is calcium, a mineral found in abundance in central Florida. When plate tectonics began ripping the supercontinent Pangaea apart late in the Paleozoic era, which spanned 540–251 million years ago, future Florida—actually part of the African continent then—got snagged like a tasty morsel in the teeth of future South and North America. Florida then sat in a warm, shallow ocean collecting the "bones" of dead marine organisms that sank to the ocean floor. This accumulated sediment would later become limestone, the only "rock" natural to Florida.

During the Cenozoic era (65.5 million years ago), Florida gradually took its current shape. Coral reefs began to form, and eroding sediment from the mainland added to the growing lump. At the end of the Oligocene epoch, sea levels dropped, and Florida emerged from the sea for the first time. Terrestrial vertebrates, including the early horse, now added their bones to the sedimentary makeup. What remained above sea level began to be affected by the acidity of rain, which dissolves soft limestone. This creation of "karst," a limerock Swiss cheese, became the storehouse for fresh water building up during this epoch. Sinkholes, caves, disappearing streams and the world-famous freshwater springs, the jewels of central Florida, were created. Nowhere else on earth are there so many artesian springs.

During the Holocene epoch (from ten thousand years ago to the present), the sea level reached its current level, and the long shape of the peninsula was set. By this time, human populations had already long been drawn to central Florida, with its underground storehouse of the freshest, clearest spring water in the world. We begin our story on this foundation of limestone and fresh spring water.

First, we must examine the engine that drives the Thoroughbred industry. Without racing, there would be no industry—a sport, perhaps, but not a big business. From a business of competition and gambling that had its roots in far older countries and cultures, the Thoroughbred racehorse had been bred for speed and stamina long before time of contact in the Americas.

Whenever two horses get together, a horse race often ensues, but as far as we know, it was Andrew Jackson, first territorial governor of the fledgling Florida and a proponent of the breeding and racing of Thoroughbreds in Tennessee and Kentucky, who is credited with first raising and racing a few horses behind the Governor's Mansion in Tallahassee in 1821. A few tracks sprang up in the frontier towns of Marianna and Calhoun between 1832 and 1848, but they were short-lived, as more "civilized" folks pouring into the new land deemed racing a public nuisance. The Seminole Wars effectively stopped racing for a while as the government of the United States attempted, unsuccessfully, to eradicate the last of the native populations east of the Mississippi.

Fort King, one of many forts erected for this purpose, became the site of future Ocala and seat of future Marion County. Ocala is an Anglicized version of a Timucuan word, *ocale*. Timucuans were the original natives from the time of contact but were gone by the time the Seminoles—several native cultures fleeing habitat encroachment in the northern colonies—moved south to fill the vacuum left by the original natives. William Bartram wrote about the success of the Seminoles on the Alachua plain (just north of Ocala), with their great herds of cattle and "squadrons of the beautiful, fleet Seminole horse."

Veterans from the Seminole Wars brought their families back to homestead the lush, tropical earth they had seen, and the face of Florida changed again. Because of the ridge of limestone running south out of Tallahassee, central Florida is higher, with better drainage, than much of the rest of the state, while the wealth of fresh water added to the attraction. At the first meeting of the assembly when Florida became a state in 1845, Marion County was named after a man who was a hero to the many South Carolinians settling in the area: General Francis Marion.

Heavily agricultural from the start, early crops included sugar cane, tobacco, rice and cotton, along with cattle and working horses. It quickly became second in population only to Leon County around the burgeoning capital of Tallahassee. By the mid-1800s, the popular Silver Springs site, the largest spring in the world, was attracting tourists from all over the world to view the amazing crystalline waters. From 1908 into the 1920s, the popular county fair brought a version of horse racing to central Florida, although a nationwide law soon declared gambling (and therefore racing) a public nuisance.

With its strong focus on agriculture, Florida from the early to mid-1920s was in the midst of a land boom. Cattle and tree harvesting (the turpentine industry) were strong additions to the agricultural products. In the 1800s, phosphate was discovered in Marion and Polk Counties. This phosphate is the purest in the world, 99 percent calcium carbonate.

James H. Bright was the instigator of the land boom in the Miami area. He had a dream that went beyond just money. He and his brother began buying up land all over the Everglades. It was he who introduced the hardy Brahma cattle to the state, one of the few breeds able to withstand the heat and humidity of south Florida. He formed a friendship and partnership with Glenn Hammond Curtis, one of the first builders of airplanes for the United States government. Together they bought up all the land around Hialeah, Opa-Locka, Miami Springs and Lake Okeechobee. It was the first huge act of land speculation in south Florida. Then they hired a young lawyer, Dan Chappell, to be their secretary and soon set about, with a few other wealthy folks, establishing a racetrack.

Bright, called the "Father of the Racing Industry in Florida," loved the ponies. Through his dedicated efforts, the Miami Jockey Club held its first meet at Hialeah Race Track on January 15, 1925.

Parimutuel gambling had yet to be legalized; nonetheless, four tracks had strong footholds in the Tampa and Miami areas by 1925, establishing the racing industry once and for all as something that would not go away. This,

Hialeah Race Track stadium in 1925. *Courtesy Coady Photography/Hialeah archives.*

in turn, attracted some of the wealthiest people in the United States to invest in Florida, including Baron C. Collier, John D. Rockefeller, Henry Ford and Harvey Firestone, all of whom commissioned the purchase of millions of acres of raw Florida land, contributing to a land boom that corrupted politicians and bankers alike. Money poured into what was then called the Palm Tree State. The powers that be ensured that the tax laws encouraged this flood, with no inheritance tax and no income tax. A state law denoting a forty-five-mile-per-hour speed limit was established; it was illegal for any municipality to enforce anything below twenty-five miles per hour. This was the fastest speed limit in the United States. Thus was the stage set in the land of speed for the conception and birth of a racehorse industry.

By the time the land boom began slowing, Bright was well established. The colorful tale, including the legalizing of parimutuel and the story of an entire society built around the flamboyance of racing in the tropics, is told in greater detail in the book *Florida Thoroughbred*.

By 1925, Ocala, the geographical center of Florida, was considered the most progressive town in central Florida. Marion County was the center of most of the state's agriculture and the intersection of new railroad lines. But following the Depression, Florida, like every other state, was desperate for revenue. On June 3, 1931, and over the double veto of Governor Doyle Carlton, the state legislature legalized parimutuel wagering so that it could be taxed as a means of raising revenue. Despite a Category 4 hurricane roaring through south Florida on September 17 and 18, the first legal horse

Gulfstream Park inaugural meeting, December 1, 1944. Doug Donn and Stefan Zachar are in the center, back row, in dark suits. *Courtesy Stefanie Zachar.*

race in the state was run at 2:32 p.m. on Saturday, December 26, 1931, at Tropical Park, which had just been converted from a dog track. Gulfstream was built in 1939 and then closed after three days of operation. James Donn revived it in 1945, and it has operated successfully since.

Because the racetracks and the racing aficionados were in south Florida, that is where the first breeding attempts took place. Bright pointed out the stamina and strength of the cow ponies, wondering why good racehorses couldn't be raised as well. He boldly stated to Bluegrass breeders on their own turf (in Kentucky) that one day Florida would raise racehorses as good as any in Kentucky. Once the ensuing laughter died down, some wit yelled out that he ought to stick to raising rattlesnakes and alligators and let Kentucky raise the nation's racehorses. Uncle Jimmy Bright refused to give up. He could see the quality of the stock—all kinds of stock—being raised in Florida and saw no reason why racehorses couldn't be one of those animals.

Bright was one of the first to recognize that one of the reasons for the sturdy livestock was that the animals could exercise and absorb sunshine year round. He began Bright's Ranch near Hialeah and, later, Martha Bright Ranch (named for his daughter) in Davie, a little farther north. There he raised the first Florida-bred racehorses as early as 1925, even as he was fighting for legalized parimutuel wagering. Those early endeavors resulted in horses that weren't even registered with the Jockey Club Thoroughbred Registry of America, but a few became mighty fine polo ponies. His Martha's

Mucho Gusto at Golden Shoe Farm in 1944. *Courtesy Stefanie Zachar.*

Queen, foaled in 1936, became the first Florida-foaled horse registered with the Jockey Club. After several attempts on the track, Martha's Queen also became the first Florida-bred to win a race in 1939. When one of his other horses also won a small race, the first recognized Florida-bred horses earned a whopping total of $675 their first year of racing.

The well-known architect and racetrack promoter Stefan Zachar also did some breeding at his Golden Shoe Farm, near Davie. The Zachars were the first to stand a major stakes winner in Florida, Mucho Gusto.

By 1946, there were enough Florida-foaled youngsters to hold a restricted race (open only to Florida horses). Although uncommon at the time, it was not unheard of to give a head start to a new industry. However, the regular jockeys refused to ride what they considered pint-sized horses, and the track announcer refused to call the races. Mrs. Stefan Zachar, herself a strong advocate of racing and breeding, became the first female race announcer in the nation when she called the first race ever held solely for Florida-foaled horses.

On January 21, the race took place on the new Nursery Course at Hialeah. This was a three-furlong chute leading straight onto the track so that the green babies would not have to negotiate a turn. Three Florida-breds were from Broward County, one from Dade County and one from Duval County.

As one jockey was boosted into the saddle, he looked around and muttered, "There ain't much to hang on to, is there?"

That filly, Sweet Hash, won the race. Bright told anyone who would listen that soon there would be enough Florida horses to hold a stakes race strictly for horses bred in Florida. Two years later, that would come true.

A few more racing aficionados joined those first southern breeders, including wealthy car dealers Mr. and Mrs. Tilyou Christopher, who built Christopher Ranch near what is today Miami International Airport. They were among the first to make the difficult choice of keeping their good racehorse, Doublerab, in Florida as a stud instead of sending him to Kentucky, where stud fees and mare pedigrees would have been better.

Those first southern-bred animals indeed tended to be puny; it was guessed that some supplement was needed—it really was sandy soil after all. So, several things were tried to increase their stature. The Christophers tried raising their early foals on goats' milk. Despite the laughter regarding the "goat foals," they still ran.

Gradually, however, despite these early successes, folks began to realize that south Florida really did lack that something that imparted the solid, flat bone and stamina that was the hallmark of a good racehorse. They won, seemingly "outrunning their pedigrees"—which was a phrase that would be repeated over the next decade—and they were tough, but those kinds of horses, while stimulating some grudging admiration, weren't ever going to be the foundation of an industry. Something more was needed.

Chapter 2

THE LEXINGTON OF FLORIDA

W hen Florida bumped into the North American continent, and its ridged backbone lifted above the ocean surface, it began absorbing and storing a finite supply of fresh water in a unique limestone formation with holes and caverns. Florida is essentially an aquifer with a thin—and not always stable—crust of limestone on top. "It's in the water" and "It's in the soil" were heard often in the early days of the industry, spoken by out-of-state head-scratchers.

Why do we care about a geology lesson in a book about Thoroughbred racehorses? Limestone and horses are linked, and not just because limestone grows strong bones. The man who today is called the "Father of the Florida Thoroughbred Industry" is also called the "Father of the Limerock Industry." The Carl G. Rose Highway, running through the middle of Ocala and Marion County, is just one of the memorials left in his wake. In a way, all of Florida's highways are a memorial.

Carl was born the son of Graham Rose in Bourbon, Indiana, the importer of many fine draft horses from Germany, Belgium, England and France; this instilled an early love of horses in his son. Carl moved to east Florida with his wife, Ann, and one-year-old son, Graham, in 1916 to be the superintendent of a construction company that had the contract to build the first asphalt road in Florida. Building roads on shifting sands was a unique challenge that no one had yet resolved. Many substrates, including oyster shells and Indian mound materials, had been used as road bases to varying degrees of dissatisfaction and durability.

After testing a number of materials, Rose learned of the limestone ridge running down the center of the state. He had it tested for purity and then won the right to use it as a road substrate material. Rose fell in love with the high, dry, rolling hills of Marion County and moved his small family there in 1918. He began buying thousands of acres at five to ten dollars per acre. He ran cattle and other animals on much of Rosemere Farm and then began to entice new settlers to the area, selling his five-dollar acres for a good bit more. He became very active as a civic-minded citizen in his county, helping develop several industries and creating many charity organizations.

He made friends with Dave Scholtz, who became governor of Florida in January 1933. Later that year, Scholtz replaced the old racing commission with his own supporters and asked Rose to fill one of the vacancies. This was clearly a case of favoritism since Rose had nothing to qualify him except having traveled through the Bluegrass State on his move to Florida. But Ocala residents applauded the move. Rose had not, to this point, been to a racetrack or a horse farm, but he attacked the idea with characteristic enthusiasm. He was credited with cleaning up some of the shadier sides of the racing industry and, in the process, met Jimmy Bright and the southern breeders.

Bright encouraged him to get involved with breeding. Rose knew from his father's equine endeavors the importance of calcium in raising livestock. He was already successful with his cattle-raising endeavors, and he enjoyed racing his cow ponies against anyone willing to compete.

His interest was also piqued by the Kentuckians' claims of their state being the only possible location to raise a decent racehorse, so he dove in. He bought an unsuccessful racing mare from a disgusted Marshall Field (magnate of the Chicago department stores), who informed him that the mare could not be trained. Rather than train her, Rose entered her into a new career of popping out babies that could be trained. Jacinth became Rose's foundation mare, producing fourteen foals, all of which would become winners. In 1939, the same year Florida had its first winner, Rosemere Rose was the first registered Thoroughbred dropped in Marion County. She was also Rose's first Thoroughbred to hit the track, but she would not be his first winner.

Like Bright, Rose readily admitted that one reason he began promoting the Thoroughbred industry was to sell the many acres of real estate he owned. But he was also hooked. He soon became passionate about the raising and breeding of good racehorses.

Rose astonished his neighbors when he purchased another seven hundred acres from a cattle farmer on what is today Highway 200 for the unheard-of price of twenty dollars per acre. This particular patch of real estate became Rolling Acres, the section of Rosemere Farm dedicated strictly to the raising of Thoroughbred racehorses, while cattle, cow ponies, goats and Tennessee Walkers were now restricted to other parts of the large farm. He told anyone who would stand still that this country had everything necessary to raise fine horses: rich, fertile soil; flowing spring water; and groves of magnolias, pines and live oaks for shade. The climate was virtually insect-free and averaged seventy-four degrees year round.

In 1940, Rose brought in the first Thoroughbred stallion to stand in the county. A product of the army's thinning of its cavalry ranks, the army remount stallion named Green Melon was a winner at Hialeah. A year later, he was replaced with another remount stallion named Suffern. In December 1943, Rose became Marion County's first breeder of a winner when Gornil, by Green Melon out of Jacinth, won a race at Tropical Park.

In 1945, most of the twenty-one breeding farms in the state were in southern Florida. Two were located near Jacksonville and one was in St. Augustine as breeders continued to seek the right combination of soil, water and climate to produce a good racehorse. Rosemere was the largest breeder. Everett Clay, Hialeah publicist and proponent of the Florida industry from

Carl Rose with Miss Helen in 1945. *Courtesy Buddy Rose.*

its earliest years, wrote in the May edition of *Florida Cattleman* that it was just a matter of time before a Florida-bred horse would take Florida's top prize, the Widener Cup Stakes, held at Hialeah at the peak of winter racing.

By the mid-1940s, Rosemere's Rolling Acres, with its active training track, was a tourist attraction and a popular local hangout. Since the track was located on a main highway near the airport, few newcomers to the area could fail to miss the morning workout excitement. On Sunday afternoons, the sheriff collected the tickets for minor betting on the racing. The Marion County Fair Association sponsored the first race meet at the Rolling Acres training track in July 1945.

Tourists who visited Rosemere Farm were inducted into the "Rosy Order of the Gate Openers." They soon discovered that it was their task to open and close the more than one thousand gates on the farm as they toured the various livestock sections. If Rose was not busy with one of his many endeavors, he enjoyed conducting the tours himself.

In July 1945, a real boost to the fledgling industry occurred when a big-name Kentucky breeder actually bought a horse bred in Florida. Rosemere Count was sold to Almahurst Farm in Kentucky, which stood three of the nation's best stallions. The local paper reported this significance as akin to "a universal demand by California for Florida citrus fruit!"

In December 1945, Rose was quoted in the local paper, the *Sentinel Star*, as noting that "Marion County's limerock will grow stronger horses faster than any spot in Florida. When enough people discover this, that $25 and $30 an acre land will jump to $100 an acre!"

Rose decided that it was time to get serious about his Thoroughbred operations. As yet, there were no truly knowledgeable horsemen in Marion County. Most horsemen were located at the tracks. So, Rose made a move that would turn the tide of the industry and the history of Marion County and Florida. He hired a veteran horseman named Elmer Heubeck of Reisterstown, Maryland, as his new farm manager.

Heubeck had grown up in the professional horse country of Maryland and Virginia and knew the industry from the bottom up. After marrying his high school sweetheart, Harriet, they moved to Hialeah, where he trained and worked under masters such as Guy Bedwell. After World War II broke out, Heubeck returned to Maryland, where he worked as farm manager for C.E. Tuttle's Glade Valley Farm. When Tuttle decided that he was going to move to Oregon, Heubeck, a brand-new father, chose not to accompany him, instead placing a work-wanted ad in *Blood Horse* magazine. When Carl Rose answered his ad, he was dubious. Like everyone else, all he'd seen of Florida was sand, ocean and palm trees. He knew well the picturesque tracks…but farm country?

Heubeck decided to take a chance and moved his small family to Florida. After one look, he very nearly turned back. "All the fencing was barbed wire; the cattle ran with the horses and there were more animals than Noah's Ark," he said in an interview in the early 1980s. "Rose liked animals! It sure didn't look like a professional thoroughbred farm."

Luckily, Heubeck also noticed the crystal-clear springs, the lush if strange bahia grass and the limestone deposits that provided a solid substrate for live oaks, with their shallow-spreading root systems, to provide ample shade in the heat of summer.

Heubeck had his work cut out for him. His first job was to convince Rose, who liked to keep things natural-looking, that barbed wire was not natural to a high-strung Thoroughbred. Boards and mesh wire gradually began to replace the barbs, and while Heubeck conceded that horses didn't need to be stalled as much in Florida as they did in the frigid North, the open sheds gradually gave way to true barns, where the work of grooming and caretaking could more easily occur.

At the time of Heubeck's arrival, Rose owned eight Thoroughbred mares and boarded another four for his good friend Charlie O'Neil, who lived in south Florida. Heubeck also began to train the three yearlings on the farm. Rose had never raced his horses himself; he bred to sell, which was unusual at that time. "Commercial" breeding was not yet a concept, as most owners bred to race. But Rose had established a pattern of selling his stock as 2-year-olds to O'Neil, who paid for them out of their ensuing purses. Once Heubeck arrived, however, more mares were bred, and they started producing more than O'Neil wanted to buy.

Rose was one of the few people guaranteed at least ten stalls during the popular Hialeah meet, so a new means of selling was developed. Horses bred and trained at Rosemere arrived at Hialeah in early spring of their 2-year-old years to race in Rose's name for the purpose of selling them. By March 1, the end of the Hialeah season, they had all been sold, either through the claiming ranks or outright. "Once potential owners saw our horses run a three furlong clip or saw their performances in their first races, we had no trouble selling them," Heubeck said.

In later years, Heubeck credited Rose with recognizing what was missing in the runtier, southern-bred stock and moving the breeding industry north to Marion County. As Kentuckians had scoffed, it really was just sand and palm trees in south Florida.

But the cattle farm was not yet "bred" out of the owner. When his cowhands ran short of cow ponies, they sometimes "borrowed" the racing stock to herd cattle on other portions of Rosemere Farm. Despite the risk, this had the welcome result of letting the young horses grow accustomed to many and varied surprises so that they were hard to frighten by the time they got to the track. The proximity of Rosemere to the local airport also prepared them for the now very large and very busy Miami International Airport near Hialeah.

But Kentuckians continued to laugh at the pedigrees, even as the poorly bred animals began to win races. Rose was not a man for putting out a lot of money for blooded stock (witness the army remount stallions). He happily received the culls of other breeders or picked up decent mares by waiting for the end of racing meets and finding owners or trainers who couldn't pay their track bills and were willing to sell cheap. After every meet, Heubeck arrived back at the farm with a vanload of new stock. Heubeck guessed that the most he ever paid for a horse on Rose's behalf was $200. And yet, win they did, to the Kentucky breeders' bafflement. One breeder finally had to admit that there had to be something in the soil since there certainly wasn't anything in the blood.

Just because he had hired a knowledgeable farm manager did not mean that Rose backed out of the operations of the farm. He continued to ride his lead pony on the tracks and walk hots and could rattle off the pedigree and racing record of any animal on his farm. He took as much interest in the people who worked for him as he did in his animals, endearing himself to all who knew him.

He was involved in the community as well. At various times, he was president of the Marion Construction Company, the Ocala Limerock Corporation, the Marion Motor Company and the Ocala Insurance Company. He was very involved in the Crippled Children's Home as well. He liked kids, and many young jockeys got their start at Rosemere Farm. Trainer Harry Trotsek began sending jockey trainees to Rosemere, recognizing the quality of their training under the Heubeck wing. Many went on to become big-name jockeys, trainers or farm managers in their own right: Manny Tortora, John Thornberry, Donny Jordan, George May, Pat Hunter and more.

Rose continued to be a realtor. He was more involved in getting people to move to Marion County than any other person or business in the 1940s and early '50s. But it went beyond just selling them the land, which was often, but not always, his to sell. He'd then help the new landowners find

Babies in training at Rosemere Farm. *Photo by Florida State News Bureau.*

well-drillers, construction folk, fence-builders and anything else they needed. "Some people thought he was too much help," Heubeck laughed.

The second annual race meet was held at Rolling Acres' track in 1946, Heubeck's first year there. Amazingly, some 3,500 people came from as far away as Tampa, Jacksonville and Miami. Besides Thoroughbred races, there were quarter horse races and riderless races for the young, as-yet-unbroken horses shooed down a fenced lane. A match race between Ariel Game and a quarter horse was popular. Ariel Game, owned by O'Neil, won by a nose. He would soon become an important stallion for early Florida breeders.

The year 1946 was the first that "Florida-bred" and Marion County became joint concepts in national racing circles. Rosemere Dee and Rosemere Sis won three races between them at Monmouth Park in New Jersey. Rose was invited to Garden State Race Track, where he was publicly recognized for his breeding successes. Although southern breeders also won some national races, it was Rosemere Farm that was chosen to be the site where five scenes from *The Yearling*, starring Gregory Peck, Jane Wyman and Claude Jarman Jr., were shot. Reporters began coming to the farm to shoot pictures and show the modern luxuries of a Thoroughbred farm in Florida.

Few places anywhere in the world could rival the beauty and the lush, rolling pastures of Rosemere Farm.

This was the heyday of racing. *Blood Horse* magazine reported that "nowhere had it seen such a madhouse as Miami was, with gambling and inflation running riot; hotels an outrageous $20 a night."

When Rosemere-bred horses had won $32,775 by mid-September 1946, Rose turned his limestone operations over to his oldest son, Graham, in favor of spending more time with his horse business. He was selling chunks of old Rosemere then for $200 per acre, more than doubling even his own dreams. By November, Rose was being quoted in the *Sentinel Star*, "We're waiting for the day when a Florida bred and trained horse wins the Kentucky Derby or some other big stakes race. Then our new industry will be over the hump."

Just two months later, in December 1946, Mrs. Christopher's Donna's Ace became the first Florida-foaled horse to win a stakes race when she tromped a competitive field in the $10,000 added Ponce de Leon Handicap at Tropical Park.

Florida breeding was now an established concept, if a fluctuating location. About eighty Florida Thoroughbreds campaigned around the nation's racetracks, winning an unexpected $66,810 by the end of 1946. They were proving that they were viable competition if not yet the high-end winners. Ten stallions stood in the state, and Rosemere Farm sold the first Florida-foaled horse ever sold at a public auction in the fall Kentucky yearling sales for a respectable $3,000. The local papers noted that the filly looked better than many of her Kentucky counterparts.

In the fall of 1947, Rose was advised that he had been approved for another remount stallion named *Samurai. (The asterisk indicated a foreign-bred horse in bygone days; today, the country of origin is noted instead.) *Samurai, a prize of war taken during World War II, was the product of Adolph Hitler's breeding program for superhorses. He was of the finest bloodlines Germany had to offer and was considered the best horse ever to come out of Germany. However, in the chaos of war, his papers had been lost, so the Jockey Club refused to recognize his bloodlines. Instead, it stamped his foals' papers with "For racing purposes only." His first progeny hit the races in 1953 and ran so well that the Jockey Club was forced to erase the blemish on the pedigrees halfway through the year. *Samurai would continue to be influential to the early breeding program in Florida.

Rose was dubbed the "man who brought Kentucky to Florida." Even past scoffers had to agree that the ability to train year round and leave horses out of doors in the sunshine and warmth must count for something. Elmer

Organizational meeting of the FTBA in Miami, September 1945. *Front row, left to right*: Mr. and Mrs. Davis Nosek, Carl Rose and Dr. C.C. Collins. *Standing*: C.A. O'Neil, Dr. T.H. Yarborough, Dan Chappell, C. Burlinghame, Hunter Lyon, Stefan Zachar and Dr. George E. Woolard. *Courtesy Buddy Rose.*

Heubeck predicted that soon, many northerners would begin shipping their horses to Florida to train, even if they didn't want to breed there.

In an effort to formalize the budding industry, nine Florida breeders, from both south and central Florida, met on September 11, 1945, to create the Florida Thoroughbred Breeders' Association. The story of the FTBA is the story of the industry. It was the organization's job to assist the breeders as it moved forward with cutting-edge programs, ideas and lobbies for better legislation, up to the present day.

Those nine people chose eleven people to be the first directors of the new organization. Jimmy Bright was made president, Carl Rose vice-president, Stefan Zachar secretary and Charles O'Neil treasurer. Attorney Dan Chappell prepared the constitution and charter and would later be voted president, a position he held until 1957. When he died in 1981, he was the last surviving member of the eleven original board members. During the preliminary meetings, membership fees were determined (twenty-five dollars), as were the methods of registering what would now be known as a "Florida-bred" in the new state registry. The first certificate ever issued by the group was for Franc's Cracker, foaled on February 19, 1946, and bred by Hunter Lyon. The cost to register a foal was two dollars.

Two rules were passed to encourage Florida breeding. One provided for a five-pound allowance for Florida-breds in open competition within the state. The other rule required the three major tracks pay $250 to the breeder of any Florida-bred winner. The tracks, eager to encourage the growing industry, agreed to these proposals. The new organization also became associated with the National Association of Thoroughbred Breeders in America and the National Association of Thoroughbred Clubs. It was an auspicious beginning, but it took a few years to solidify. Like the industry itself, it floated between hotels and restaurants in south Florida as meeting places, and at first, board members only met once per year. By 1951, they had taken over the awarding of breeders' awards from the tracks; they petitioned for a certain number of stalls to be reserved for Florida-breds at the tracks, and the tracks were asked to increase the number of Florida-bred restricted races.

When an out-of-state man began to take advantage of the lucrative Florida breeding program and won too many of its restricted races, he forced the fledgling organization to change its Florida-bred rules. Although this change would later be rescinded, at the time it seemed necessary and worked to encourage this man to become a Florida breeder, an excellent move for the state industry.

Thus enters the second limestone-road character. Fred Hooper grew up the son of a Georgia farmer and one of many children. He left home to become a barber and then a boxer in Alabama, where he became heavyweight champion. In 1920, he bought his first forty acres of Florida land in Palatka, planted potatoes and cabbage and then lost everything in four days when a potato blight struck. It was back to barbering again.

It was in 1926, when U.S. 1 was being built from Boston to Key West, that he got his break. While barbering the construction workers' hair, Hooper learned that both a few trucks and a contract for twenty-four miles of road were available from the trucks' owner, who couldn't pay his bills. When he dreamed that he was a contractor, he got up the next morning, went to a bank to ask for a $100,000 loan and hung up his barbering tools once and for all. He took his leap of faith.

He became known as the "Swamp Rabbit," a road construction worker blazing roads through swamps where no one else would or could go. Through the 1930s, by robbing Peter to pay Paul, Hooper built up his Hooper Construction Company until he was the largest construction company in the Southeast, with a fleet of vehicles and employees. It became the multimillion-dollar General Development Corporation. By the mid-1940s, he was a highly respected builder of roads, dams and airports. But he did not leave his farming heritage behind. When cotton farmers began going broke in Alabama, he bought up sixteen farms and turned them into pasture for the largest herd of shorthorn cattle in the Southeast. He ran cattle in Palatka as well.

Hooper had a love of horses based on his early farm experiences and had long dreamed of owning a "real" horse. In the early 1930s, Jimmy Bright sold Hooper a filly named Seminole Lady, which won many match races for him and also fired his passion for horses and speed. He then purchased a crossbred gelding from Rose that he put up against anything with four legs. In between wrangling cattle, Royal Prince won forty-nine of fifty-five starts, a record that Hooper's later bluebloods never beat. He was hooked.

But he was also busy, with little time to devote to his favorite hobby; all that hard work extracted a price. Between running the largest stock farms in the Southeast, GDC and homes all over Florida and Alabama, Hooper crashed and was forced by his doctors to take a rest. While on his enforced break, he heard of the yearling sales in Kentucky, so decided to go buy a horse.

At the sales, Hooper bumped into a smaller man who was also alone and introduced himself. Ivan Parke, a successful trainer and previous jockey, helped Hooper purchase his first quality Thoroughbreds. Hooper had also found his trainer.

Hooper named the Sir Galahad III colt Hoop Jr. and sent his new purchase off to the 2-year-old wars. By the end of five starts, the colt had won two and placed in the other three; he had some real talent. Before retiring for the season, Hooper told anyone who would listen that Hoop Jr. would win the 1945 Kentucky Derby. Everyone chuckled, tickled with the new owner's naïveté. Hoop Jr. won the 1945 Kentucky Derby. Hooper would spend the rest of his life trying to duplicate that beginner's luck feat.

Hooper also purchased his new trainer's month-old colt, considering his trainer's ownership a conflict of interest. This became Olympia, another major stakes winner and a future foundation sire for Hooper Farms.

Hooper always liked to do things his own way. One of his ways was to use the new FTBA's Florida-bred rule that a foal simply had to be born in Florida to be a Florida-bred. So, to qualify for those lighter weights and special purses at the Florida tracks, he shipped his Alabama-based mares across the border just long enough to drop their foals, brought them back to his Alabama farm and proceeded to raise "Florida-breds." They won too many of the restricted races and breeders' awards at the Florida tracks, so the breeders' organization changed the rule to require non-domiciled mares to remain in Florida long enough to be bred back to a Florida-based stallion. Although that rule held for many years, Florida breeders today no longer fear someone taking advantage of their rulings but rather welcome any and all mare owners who want to drop foals in the Sunshine State. Many breeders leave their mares anyway; it's hard to beat Florida's weather.

Hooper first tried trading mares for Florida-bred foals, but finally giving in to the old adage, "If you can't lick 'em, join 'em," he moved his whole breeding operation from Montgomery, Alabama, to Marion County in

Susan's Girl in the Delaware Handicap. *Courtesy* The Florida Horse.

Hooper and Susan's Girl, Braulio Baeza up. *Courtesy* The Florida Horse.

October 1966 and became one of the most active and influential Florida breeders from then on.

Hooper's beginner's luck continued when, in 1945, he bought his wife, Laura, a black colt by Ariel. This grew up to be Education, the nation's best 2-year-old in 1946, and assured Laura's love of the industry as well. By the time they reached Florida, the couple created His and Her, side-by-side farms. Hers was named Devotion Farm, and they built their home on it. Her

Left: Hooper and Susan's Girl as broodmare. *Photo by Charlene R. Johnson.*

Below: Precisionist in Breeders' Cup. *Courtesy* The Florida Horse.

silks—also red, white and blue—had a blue and white cap, while Hooper's silks included a blue and red cap.

Hooper's influence was felt far beyond the borders of the Sunshine State, however. His construction business became involved in track and turf construction all over the country. He was involved in the formation, in 1958, of the American Thoroughbred Owners' Association, was its first president and then, in 1961, helped transform it into today's Thoroughbred Owners' and Breeders' Association (TOBA). He was president of the FTBA from 1971 to 1979. He was one of the first breeders ever to import stallions from South America. He helped organize the Florida Stallion Stakes series in 1980. He won the Eclipse Award for Outstanding Breeder in 1975 and again in 1982. In 1991, he won the Eclipse Award of Merit for outstanding contributions to the industry.

Hooper's contributions to the industry nationwide, but especially in Florida, are endless. He produced many stakes winners, top stallions and champions. Susan's Girl was not only a Hooper favorite but also a favorite of everyone. A big, classy chestnut filly with a flashy white blaze, she earned the 3-year-old Filly Championship in 1972. She raced through six years of age, beating males and earning two Champion Handicap mare honors in 1973 and 1975. She became a great broodmare for Hooper, producing many stakes winners, including Copelan.

Of the hundreds of horses that carried the famous red, white and blue silks with the Circle H on the chest, Precisionist may have been Hooper's best. He could run short or long; he won seventeen stakes and was stakes-placed fourteen times. He earned more than $1 million in both 1985 and 1986 and was Champion Sprinter of 1985. Precisionist became Florida's leading money winner at that time with earnings of $3,485,398.

By the time Hooper died at 102 in 2000, he had bred more than one hundred stakes winners. He never again won the Kentucky Derby, but he won everything else. Like many a horseman before him, he died after watching one of his 2-year-olds work out on the track. A dispersal of all his breeding stock, weanlings, yearlings and 2-year-olds had just been announced the week before. At present, 400 acres of the old Hooper Farm form the Nelson Jones Farms and Training Center, while the remainder of the 734 acres has been turned into mini farms. Hoop Jr.'s gravestone is still on the main farm.

THE ADVENT OF RACING and breeding in Florida had already changed the Thoroughbred industry on a national level. The concept of year-round racing and the concept of early 2-year-old racing only came about because of Floridian activities. Both were the result of horses being able to stay outside year round, exercising, training, growing and overall developing faster than horses forced to find shelter for the winter. It made sense that such a horse would have an advantage for early racing. Therefore, now that facilities were growing available, as predicted, trainers began shipping their charges to farms and training facilities in Florida for the winter. Florida's rival in this field was California; both had firmly established training horses arriving from all over the United States for winter training and racing.

The Widener Cup Handicap was created in 1936 at Hialeah specifically to rival the Santa Anita Handicap in California. It was *the* winter race; both were ten years old in 1947. The March 16, 1942 issue of *TIME* magazine noted that "nearly every glamor horse in the U.S. was entered in Florida's Widener Handicap, richest race of the winter season." By 1949, four of the five divisional champions of the nation were wintering over at Hialeah.

In 1947, Florida-breds won fifty races at recognized tracks in the United States. In June of that year, Charles Gregg of *Turf and Sport Digest* wrote, "Of the 36 home-breds sent up to the racing wars thus far, 31 have triumphed in open competition. And that, viewed from any angle is some sort of record."

On February 6, 1948, Florida breeders got their first Florida-bred stakes race. Aptly named the Florida Breeders' Stakes, it was held at Hialeah and had seven entries: three from Broward County, three from Dade County and one from Marion County—Suffazon, bred by Rose and owned by Charles O'Neil. A number of famous sportswriters were on hand by special invitation, along with 13,841 fans. This race became an annual event, renamed in 1963 the Carl Rose Stakes. In the early days, the Dade County breeders dominated, especially the Christophers, but by the mid-1950s, the balance of power had swung to Marion County. Eight of the first twelve winners were foaled in Marion County.

When the 1949 Hialeah meet opened, Heubeck took ten of Rose's horses to the track for sale. By the end of the meet, not only had he sold out his entire crop in record time, but Rose's breeding operation also showed a profit for the first time. Six of them were sold to owners outside the state. When Heubeck's own Florida-bred, Werwolf, sold for an unbelievable $12,500 to a New Yorker, a prophetic line appeared in the *Miami Herald*: "Don't be surprised if Ocala becomes the Lexington of Florida."

Werwolf won the second Florida Breeders' Stakes. His new owner also purchased a Rosemere-bred and prepared to ship her two new charges to California, prompting *Blood Horse* to write, "She is certainly a brave woman…if one of these should win a stakes on the west coast, she'd need a body guard." Many commented that this was the best-looking crop of Florida-breds yet, large and healthy looking. No excuses need be made.

The year 1950 was a pivotal one for the fledgling industry. The FTBA now had fifty-four members. Oak Lane Farm, owned by J.E. Hardy, became the second farm in the county to raise Thoroughbreds (though never many), and a third Marion County farm was just being established, Dickey Leach Stables.

William E. Leach was a Miami contractor who owned a racing stable and participated in the management of Gulfstream Park. He wanted to shift his headquarters to Marion County, so purchased his first 153 acres of choice land from Rose and named it Dickey Leach Stables for his wife, whose maiden name was Dickey. He quickly built fences and a training track and brought Jack Little, former manager of Christopher Ranch, up to run the showplace farm. He accumulated eighteen Thoroughbreds, including two stallions, and opened up for boarding, training and breeding. He bought up more tracts of land and soon rivaled Rosemere, which had dwindled in size over the years, as the largest farm in Marion County.

By May 1950, "cracker thoroughbreds," as they were being called, had already earned $100,000, with fifteen juveniles already winners, five of them stakes winners, a percentage unequalled by any other state. The Christophers' Liberty Rab set a track record for three furlongs at Gulfstream. But the biggest racing upset of the year was when Liberty Rab beat undefeated blueblood hero Battlefield in the Belmont Juvenile Stakes, for an instant becoming the world's leading, money-winning juvenile for 1950 with $33,312 in earnings. He would not hold that record, as Battlefield would sweep on to more victories and the juvenile championship for the year, but ecstatic Florida breeders hooted that Battlefield had been wintered over in Florida.

Throughout 1950, baby crackers continued to make headlines. Rose persuaded four new breeders to purchase land near Rosemere and then helped them build barns, paddocks and homes. While these newcomers would never make a name as breeders, they nonetheless contributed to the growing impression of Kentucky come to Florida with their picturesque farms.

Rosemere Farm, Dickey Stables and Oak Lane Farm became the subjects of formal tours for the tourists, who began arriving by the busload. The road and fence line along the training track were constantly packed with stopped cars and rubberneckers.

By November 1950, twenty-two Rosemere horses had been shipped to Hialeah for training, racing and selling and brought an average price of $10,000, double that of most farm-sold youngsters. Five of the top ten Florida-breds for 1950 came from Rosemere, and $102,652 of the total of $282,075 total earnings by Florida-breds was Rosemere-bred earnings. By 1954, Hialeah had clapped a lid on its highly coveted stalls, and Rose was allotted only sixteen. But his horses sold so fast that he just kept refilling the stalls.

By 1951, racing was considered one of the most important industries in the state. Florida was the only state to aid education through its racetracks and gambling bills. When a Rosemere-bred named Game Gene won a race by seven lengths in early 1952 and was promptly purchased for $20,000, he set a record price for a Florida-bred. The next year, Oclirock, another Rosemere-bred, sold for $30,000, establishing yet another record. Rosemere Farm had come a long way from its first sale of $275. That winter of 1951–52, seven yearlings were shipped from Kentucky farms to train and winter over at Rosemere. This was the beginning of a new trend. Marion County was becoming recognized as a great training and lay-up center.

On January 6, 1952, Hialeah hosted the first "Baby Show" of Florida-bred yearlings. This became an annual event, judged by some of the best horsemen in the world, including Horatio Luro, James Fitzsimmons, Sherrill Ward, Ben Jones and many more. This first one was judged by Lexington trainer Preston Burch. He pinned the blue on Jimmy Bright's Florida Flash for Best Colt and Rosemere's Ari Gold for Best Filly. The second year of the show, Rosemere captured Best Colt, Filly and Gelding, as well as Best of Show.

By 1953, Rosemere stood six stallions. His farm produced six stakes winners that same year, and he was made a lifetime member of the FTBA. Besides helping others get started, Rose spent money on his own new and upgraded facilities. His barns ran east–west to take advantage of the prevailing breezes, and in 1954, he introduced creosote paint for fencing. Not only was it easier to keep up than the traditional white boards, but cribbing horses detested the taste of it. It soon spread to Kentucky. He also worked closely with the University of Florida regarding which grasses grew the best and needed which supplements. They had long ago realized that the famous Kentucky bluegrass was simply not hardy enough for the harsher conditions of Florida. His lush fields now produced bales of pangola, Pensacola bahia and alyce clover. The breeding industry of Florida would never again be held back by lack of knowledge of nutrients in the soil.

Baby Show at Hialeah. *Courtesy Coady Photography/Hialeah archives.*

The land around Rosemere was now selling for $600 per acre. Although Kentuckians still maintained that by adulthood, horses all looked pretty much the same, they had to concede that the youngsters growing up in Florida grew fatter faster and were able to race earlier than those grown in other parts of the country.

In 1955, Rose became the first breeder of a single animal bred in Florida to win more than $100,000, Marked Game. When the colt won the Christmas Handicap and raised his earnings to $108,225 for the year, it marked a triumphant finish not just to the year but also to the previous thirty years of endeavor on the part of Florida breeders. They had proven their point: Florida *could* raise a good racehorse.

Chapter 3

THE LAND THE HORSE BUILT

In 1955, FTBA members discussed the creation of a magazine to support their fledgling industry. A subcommittee was formed consisting of mostly Marion County members to continue the discussion. They planned a July 15 meeting in Ocala, which was the handwriting on the wall. Some disgruntlement had begun between northern and southern factions, such that by 1957, reorganization was discussed. What happened between 1955 and 1957 was one of those pivotal points at which an industry is made.

It is often said that Needles sold more real estate in Marion County than any realtor. At the beginning of 1956, there were 33 stallions and 199 mares on twenty-two Thoroughbred farms in the state, only four of which were in Marion County: Rosemere, Dickey Leach Stables, Oak Lane and a new one established in 1954, Douglas and Margaret Stewart's Shady Lane Farm. Although it showed little growth in farms from the twenty-one in 1946, the horse numbers had increased dramatically.

When Leach continued to bring in excellent pedigrees, including four top-grade stallions, it prompted Milton Plumb to write in an article in the *Tampa Sunday Tribune*: "A few more like these and the Bluegrass won't have a thing on Marion County."

Mary Madeline (Dickey) Leach loved the farm and the horses. She often spent weeks there while her husband remained in south Florida working. She conducted the FTBA-sponsored tours of the farm herself. The Leaches sent their first home-bred crop off to the races in 1953, a crop whose bloodlines, appearance and condition were rivaled by none, including Rosemere.

Shady Lane Farm. *Photo by Jim Jernigan.*

Three of the Leach mares had come to the farm following a convoluted partnership that split up when Leach insisted that he wanted them stabled at his farm and the foals raised as Florida-breds. Before arriving at their new home, Noodle Soup, a mare with unimpressive bloodlines and a less impressive race record, was bred by sheer luck to the 1949 Kentucky Derby

Noodle Soup and Needles. *Painting by Angie Draper.*

winner, Ponder, only because he had retired too late in the season to get a full book. Noodle Soup would produce one of only four foals in his first crop. Two of them would become champions.

On April 29, 1953, she dropped her bay colt with a white star and two short stockings. At about five weeks of age, the colt contracted equine pneumonia, often a fatal disease, and ran a high fever for weeks. Not only was this the first battle of his life, but it was also early proof of how much heart, determination and character he had. Madeline Leach, a trained nurse, worked with the farm manager, Roy Yates, and a local vet, Dr. W. Reuben Brawner, to administer one shot after another, along with doses of oxygen. Feeling sorry for all the puncturing, she named the colt Needles.

He blossomed into such a good-looking colt that a reporter took note of him his yearling year, suggesting that he could be worth watching in the future. Yet he started out a somewhat lazy animal, working only when he felt like it. His exercise boy often had to hammer heels into belly to get him to work at all. But when he finally deigned to run late in his yearling year, he impressed his onlookers.

Needles, along with the rest of the 1953 crop, was shipped to trainer Elmo Shropshire at Hialeah. Following Rosemere's lead, Dickey raced the babies to sell. Trainer and judge Sherrill Ward pinned the blue on Needles at the annual Baby Show.

Hugh Fontaine was a retired trainer who had recently revived his own career to train for a pair of wealthy, wildcatter oilmen, with little success so far. But he had seen Needles at the farm and knew a good horse when he saw him. He arrived at the Baby Show with his reluctant owners in tow,

Heath and Dudley. *Courtesy Heath and Dudley families.*

knowing that he had one shot. While willing to look, they figured that they had wasted enough money on this tough sport and had made the decision to get out unless something positive happened soon.

Bonnie McCoy Heath and Jackson Curtis Dudley trailed dubiously after Fontaine as he led them to the training track, expounding on the appearance and athleticism of the leggy bay. The potential owners agreed that he seemed

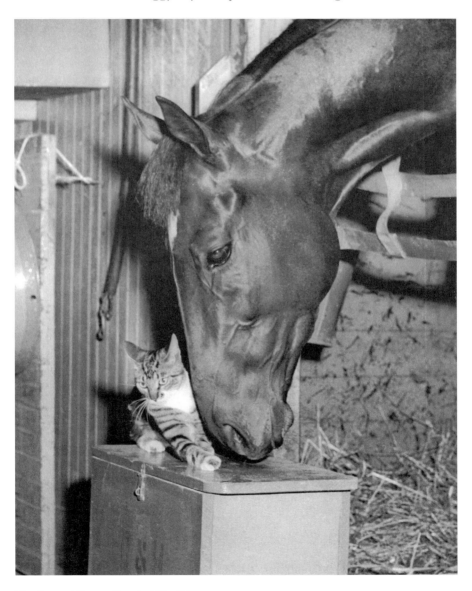

Needles and Boots. *Photo by Mike Sirico.*

to be a nice-looking colt, but the asking price of $20,000 was awfully steep, especially for a Florida-bred. It wasn't likely to drop after the colt won the beauty show.

They watched him work three-eighths of a mile, casually breaking the track record for the distance while making it look easy. Still they held back—it was a lot of money, and they had told their wives that they might buy a filly as a potential broodmare. When Fontaine begged for a loan if they wouldn't buy the colt, adding that he'd offer a mortgage on everything he owned but his wife, they decided that his faith was worth supporting. The partners soon owned a new racehorse—one that would never make a broodmare.

His first race was on March 29, 1955, at Gulfstream Park. Under the blue and orange silks of D&H Stables, he won by five lengths, missing the track record by two-fifths. He proved that he was still a baby by running wide in his next start, which was his first stakes race, but still finished a respectable fourth. As he settled, his running style developed into a speedy, bolt-to-the-front-and-stay-there style. He won his next race by three lengths and reduced the track record by one-fifth. He then won his first stakes race in

Right to left: Bonnie and Opal Heath, Jimmy Bright (in wheelchair), Liz Tippett, Carl Rose (standing directly behind Bright), Saul Silberman (in bowtie), unknown, unknown and Everett Clay, publicist for Hialeah. *Photo by Leo and Jerry Frutkoff.*

August when he was put up against two unbeaten colts in the Sapling at Monmouth Park in New Jersey. He won the Hopeful Stakes and then the Garden State Stakes while setting a track record for a mile; he then finished third to Prince John and Career Boy, the best horses in the nation. After this mercurial launching of his career, Needles was voted Champion 2-Year-Old of 1955, Florida's first National Champion. Marion County's place on the Thoroughbred map was set.

Fontaine's faith was vindicated; the wildcatters' wives, Opal Heath and Phyllis Dudley, had forgiven their husbands the purchase of yet another colt and now were having the time of their lives. Florida breeders and the whole of Marion County's population were filled with the excitement of a potential Derby horse. Needles was given a break before his important 3-year-old season, and he became the first Thoroughbred to receive a college letter when he was made an honorary member of the Letterman's Club of Oklahoma A&M, Heath's alma mater.

In January 1956, Heath and Dudley purchased a 572-acre cattle farm from the Horne brothers, with plans to turn it into their new Thoroughbred operation. Heath intended to live there while Dudley would continue to work their oil business in Oklahoma.

Bonnie Heath III laughed about his naïve father and partner at that time. "When they bought the farm, they were thinking they had a Champion colt, and when he won the Kentucky Derby, they'd have to have a place to stand him! That's why they bought the farm!" Years later, after many tough years in a tough business, the partners had a good laugh at themselves.

Meanwhile, Bill Leach's health had begun to fail, so in that same month, they sold Dickey Leach Farm to a syndicate that renamed it Ocala Stud Farms. With the purchase of these two farms, some two thousand acres were now devoted to raising Thoroughbreds in the county. "They told me the country around here would never amount to anything for breeding and training horses when I started 20 years ago," Rose exulted. "Now with these two big sales of the last few days, there's no telling how big the business might become."

Another Leach-bred, King Hairan, took the new year by storm as the hottest 2-year-old on the tracks. Another Baby Show winner, he proved that pretty is as pretty does when he took three stakes in a row, nearing track records twice. Now Florida breeders had two top home-breds to watch. Nothing could have been more exciting.

Needles's 3-year-old career began in a five-furlong race in which, to everyone's surprise, he exhibited a new running style and barely managed to

Heath Farm manager Elmo Shropshire with Heather, Bonnie and Hilary Heath. *Photo by Jim Jernigan.*

finish second. His exciting early speed as a 2-year-old had become a heart-stopping, come-from-behind style. Slow out of the gate, often dead last, only gradually would he would pick up momentum until finally, like a freight train charging downhill, he would usually (but not always) nip the leaders at the wire. Although he caused his connections near heart attacks, at least he seemed to know when it was truly a race and chose to run.

His workouts were a different story. As though he had learned the difference between money on the line and practice, he began to disdain mere workouts. Many morning reporters gleefully snapped pictures as Fontaine and stable boys chased a sluggish Needles with his new jockey and the final character of this team, David Erb, often astride pounding his sides. Some days, they just sat down and waited for Needles to decide to move; sometimes he did.

As a Florida-bred, Needles was allowed a weight concession, so he carried 117 pounds compared to the 122 of the fourteen others in the Flamingo Stakes, his next start. Because of Needles, this concession was repealed for stakes races the following year. It was a compliment: Florida-breds no longer needed a hand up. Needles again trailed most of the field, but this time he

Needles and Fontaine. *Courtesy Heath and Dudley families.*

rallied in time to win, becoming the first Florida-bred to win an important prep race for the classics.

By the time of the Florida Derby, his people had become a little more accustomed to his new style of running. Dave Erb had learned that his best bet was to let the horse run his race rather than try to push him to run in a different manner. For the first time, a Florida-bred was favored in a major stakes race. He broke dead last and slowly began to peel off the laggards. Halfway around the last turn, he was still five lengths behind the leaders. In a thrilling stretch run, he ticked off his rivals one by one and charged to the wire, dropping the track record by one-fifth of a second. This was the first $100,000 win for any Florida-bred in a single race.

They were now on the road to the most coveted racing cup in the world, the Kentucky Derby. Fontaine, proving his own unique style and babying his new star, decided not to race the horse again in the five weeks between the Florida Derby and the Kentucky Derby. This was unusual enough, but when Needles's refusal to work turned into an art form the final weeks before the Derby, many worried whether the horse would even be in shape to run. "Needles—Sharp without Sharpening" read the cover title of *Blood Horse* for May 12, 1956.

Erb knew his horse and begged Fontaine to let him work just a few days before the Derby; Needles was in the mood. But Fontaine had promised the turf writers that his star would work out the following day. Erb had to fight to hold Needles back on his chosen day to work. The next day, he was back to his usual distaste of work, with all the reporters standing witness. After a full thirty minutes of throwing dirt clods and slapping hats against thighs, Needles finally consented to work what was probably the slowest prep ever for the Kentucky Derby.

Whitney Tower explained it in his article in *Sports Illustrated* of May 7, 1956: "Needles, for instance, is not a work horse. He does not require much work to remain fit, and nobody apparently seems to be more aware of this than Needles himself, who, unless he feels like putting out in the morning, will struggle to avoid getting to the race track, or, once there against his will, take a particular delight in refusing to do what is asked of him." Tower added later in the article, "Needles was foaled in Florida (although he was conceived in Kentucky)." Never before nor since has anyone worried about where a horse was conceived. Kentuckians just couldn't allow that a Florida horse could be so good, but consultation of the Jockey Club rules stated clearly that a horse was "bred" in the state in which it was dropped, not conceived.

Bad omens seemed to continue as the entire Sunshine State, and Marion County in particular, held its collective breath the last days before the famous first Saturday in May. Dave Erb came down with a bad head cold and stayed in bed right up to the day; no horse whose name started with an *N* had ever won the Derby—speaking of which, what kind of a Derby name is "Needles" anyway? Bill Leach, his breeder, hoping to witness the race, came down with a bad case of gout and had to stay home. Of course, the biggest point of all was that no Florida-bred had ever won the Kentuckian's (or, for that matter, the nation's) premier race.

The big day arrived, and the track was fast. A Florida-bred filly named Delamar set a track record while winning the Debutante Stakes earlier in the day, setting the stage for the gleeful Florida contingent. To the astonishment of all, Needles was made the favorite.

He got off to a bad start and, on the backside, spit out the bit, refusing to run. He was second to last, twenty lengths off the leaders, when a panicky Erb, sitting tight despite an urge to push, felt his mount change his mind. By

Opposite, top: Needles wins the Kentucky Derby. *Courtesy Heath and Dudley families.*

Opposite, bottom: The happy team. *Courtesy Heath and Dudley families.*

A happy Fontaine in the center—can't stop grinning. *Courtesy Heath and Dudley families.*

the top of the stretch, he had motored into seventh place, still a daunting task for an ordinary racehorse. Some reported that it was the strongest stretch run in the history of the eighty-two-year-old Derby. When Needles charged across the finish line, ears pricked and going away, the Kentuckian's race, the racing industry and Marion County would never again be the same.

Even as the owners, trainer and groom convened on the reviewing stand to receive their trophies, a U.S. marshal strode up to serve Fontaine with papers for back income taxes. Fontaine accepted them with a grin: "That don't bother me, boy. Not today!"

While he still felt that Needles did best with long rests between races, and the Preakness was only two weeks away, Fontaine could not refuse this chance at the Triple Crown. Needles's slow-to-roll style, however, could not make up the twenty lengths he lagged in this shorter race; the distance ran out too soon. He finished second despite a valiant charge.

The longest leg of the Triple Crown, the Belmont, was three weeks later. This time, Needles pulled his stop-dead stunt right in the middle of the post parade. Gazing off into the crowds as though to evaluate whether this was the real deal or not, no one could get him to move. Finally, he dropped his

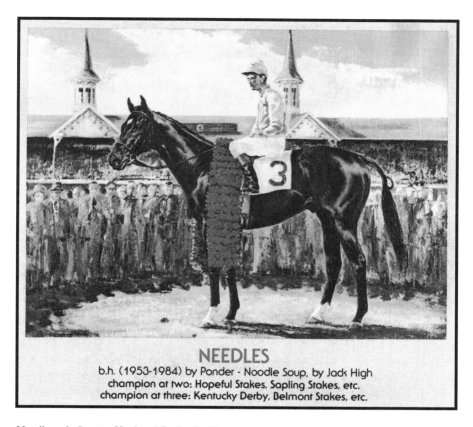

NEEDLES
b.h. (1953-1984) by Ponder - Noodle Soup, by Jack High
champion at two: Hopeful Stakes, Sapling Stakes, etc.
champion at three: Kentucky Derby, Belmont Stakes, etc.

Needles ad. *Courtesy Heath and Dudley families.*

head and strode into the gate as though he had planned to all along. Once again, he was dead last. He didn't make his move until the half-mile pole, a heart-rendingly long time to wait. Finally charging for the wire, he surged ahead by a mere neck over the failing Career Boy.

His last two races of the year were not good performances, and it soon became apparent that he had been injured. He retired for the year with earnings of $440,850 and the national 3-Year-Old Colt Championship. He was also the leading money winner of the year, while King Hairan was the leading stakes winner of the year. For the first time, Florida-breds went over the million-dollar mark with $1,459,791, nearly doubling the previous year's earnings.

Before, it had only seemed like a lot of tourists came to Marion County to see Rosemere and the other farms. Now it was a flood. They came by the busloads, not to see Silver Springs or the Ocala National Forest but rather to

Needles on eve of Belmont. *Courtesy* The Florida Horse.

see Needles, the Florida-bred winner of the Kentucky Derby, symbol of all possibilities. Billboards outside town loudly proclaimed Ocala his home and even gave directions to the farm.

At about this time, Heath and Dudley decided to form two separate farms. Dudley's son, Scott, would manage the Dudley farm, while Heath would remain actively involved in his own farm most of his life. Both second generations—Scott Dudley and his wife, Diane, and Bonnie Heath III and his wife, Kim—would continue to be actively involved in the industry into the 2000s.

Bonnie Heath (the original) was as involved in the community as Rose before him. Among much other charity work, he helped unite many different charity organizations into the United Appeal in 1961. He was the organization's first president. Its name was soon changed to United Way. He called this his proudest accomplishment until the day of his death on November 4, 2001, at the age of eighty-five—at which time, like Carl Rose, he also had a highway named after him, a portion of Silver Springs Boulevard.

Jack and Phyllis Dudley. *Courtesy Heath and Dudley families.*

Two generations of Heaths in 1994. *Photo by Louise E. Reinagel, courtesy Heath and Dudley families.*

Ocala Stud was now the owner of Noodle Soup, having inherited the mares with the farm when it bought Dickey Leach Stables. Strangely, Ponder was notably unavailable for a repeat booking to him. A school contest held to name Needles's latest half sibling was won by a Miami schoolgirl with the name Sky High. Needles was invited to Gainesville for half-time of the big game between the University of Florida and the University of Miami, and the chamber of commerce made Needles an honorary member, while Ocala handed the key to the city to its equine star.

Although his 4-year-old year would not be as flamboyant as his 2- or 3-year-old years, Needles went out with a typical blaze of glory when he equaled the track record in the Fort Lauderdale Handicap at Gulfstream Park. He ended his racing career with twenty-one starts, eleven wins, three seconds, three thirds and earnings of $600,355.

After serious soul-searching and equally serious offers from Kentucky to stand Needles in the Bluegrass, where the money and higher-quality mares would have benefitted the stallion, Heath and Dudley decided to support their new home and made the tough decision to keep Needles in Florida as a stud. "We bought the land here because we are interested in the Florida

Needles. *Courtesy Heath and Dudley families.*

program," Heath said in an interview in 1983. "But there is no question that as a stallion, Needles would have made more of a name for himself in Kentucky. Still, his 13 percent average of stakes winners is no slouch."

In 2013, Diane Dudley Parks said, "Until Dudley and Heath made a big financial sacrifice by keeping Needles in Florida—and it was a sacrifice for the horse too—I think without that giant step we might never have gotten much further. Someone else would have done it eventually, but it was them who made the sacrifices. That was a highly courageous point in the industry."

He had become a legend in Marion County. Needles was the first four-legged to be inducted into Florida's Sports Hall of Fame. Yet still the blueblood breeders held out; despite nominations year after year, it would be the year 2000 before Needles would finally be accepted into the national Racehorse Hall of Fame, in the category of Horse of Yesteryear for horses raced more than twenty-five years earlier. By the time Needles was inducted, Bonnie Heath III guessed that he was still the only horse to have received athletic letters from two universities.

The stories of his character continued. He was a ham for the camera; he loved to look gentle and kind, stick out his tongue to be stroked and then gradually pull it in until he could nip unsuspecting fingers. Schoolchildren of Marion County were bussed out to the Heath farm, where they might run around the training track and meet the old equine star. Needles lived to be thirty-one years old, a star in many eyes to the day he died.

By 1957, the impact of this new industry had become a glimmer in the politician's eye. Governor Leroy Collins stated that he recognized the economic and jobs impact this industry had on the state. He made a special trip to New York just to invite racehorse owners to move their stables to Florida.

Marion County was dubbed the "Kingdom of the Sun" and boasted fifteen thousand inhabitants. Needles had boosted the number of Thoroughbred farms in the county from four to seven by the end of 1956, but within just one year, that number tripled to twenty-one, a growth rate unsurpassed anywhere in the world. New barns, fencing and improved pasturage rapidly spread across the land once popular for cattle and agriculture. A Kentuckian, Tom M. Daniels, sold his Lexington farm, Broadmoor, and moved his operation to Marion County, citing to questioning reporters that Kentucky was becoming too industrialized and that Florida was obviously the place to raise and train horses year round.

In the spring of 1957, Grant Dorland, who already owned two farms named Roseland in Kentucky, purchased a 120-acre cattle ranch near Ocala and started Roseland number three. Convinced by Carl Rose that Florida was the place to raise a good racehorse, he then sold off his northern farms and concentrated on Marion County. He readily admitted that neither of his Kentucky farms would be considered "showplaces," but by the time he had developed his Florida land one year later, he told reporters that it was something out of a picture. "The beautiful trees are what make the Ocala farms stand out," he said in October 1958. "All of these trees grow to tremendous heights, similar to those in Saratoga and most of them are festooned with Spanish moss. Here and there are huge magnolias which grow just as tall as any of the others. A well-ordered thoroughbred farm in this section actually looks more like a park."

He went on to talk about one mare from his Kentucky farms that always looked poorly and remained barren year after year, but once she was moved to Florida, she bloomed and promptly got in foal.

In 1961, P.A.B. Widener, grandson of Hialeah's Widener, purchased 6,700 acres, some of which he developed into Live Oak Plantation. Dan Chappell, the lawyer who had gotten parimutuel passed, moved north to start Sunshine Stud. Impressed by this sudden growth of farms, several writers referred to the area as the "Land the Horse Built" or the "County the Horse Built."

One of the key factors in the early development of the industry in Florida was a successive string of men who enthusiastically and effectively marketed the idea of racing and breeding in Florida: Bright in the south and Rose in Marion County, followed by Heath, who was equally vocal. However, Marion County was about to learn the definition of salesman.

Chapter 4

A HALF CENTURY OF QUALITY

Today, in 2014, there is exactly one historic Thoroughbred farm still operating, still running strong, still in the same location and still run by the same surname that has been attached to it from the beginning. While a few second- and third-generation horsemen and horsewomen are carrying on their predecessors' efforts, only this original, early farm remains.

As of 2014, Ocala Stud consists of three farms totaling five hundred acres in Marion County. The main farm and office on the original location also still sport the same training track—maintained up to modern day standards—created some sixty years earlier. The farm is run by not just the second but also the third and fourth generations of the man who is credited with starting it. Its website states, "A Half Century of Quality," but it's actually more than that.

Ocala Stud bred and sold more than one hundred stakes winners, most of which are by Ocala Stud sires, including one Horse of the Year. It also stood Florida's Champion Sire nine times just since 2000. In 2013, Ocala Stud was named national Breeder of the Year. It won this honor by earning $3,153,794 for the calendar year of 2012, with five stakes winners, a sixth bred in partnership, and with Musical Romance being named the national Champion Female Sprinter for 2012. This is only the latest of the legacy of Ocala Stud Farms.

Although the original purchase of the Dickey Leach farm was not made solely with O'Farrell's dollars, history proves nonetheless that the success of Ocala Stud is due to him. In the beginning, it was Bruce C. Campbell, a

Marylander who had made a small fortune in the ready-mix concrete business, who first saw the ad for Dickey Stables somewhere called Ocala, Florida. Already a racing aficionado with a winter home in Miami, he was ready to do something more than just race a horse or two. On January 15, 1956, he called his friend, Joseph Michael O'Farrell, and his own son, McLean ("Mack"), and asked them to meet him in Ocala to assess the property.

Joe O'Farrell left the snow of Maryland and arrived in the county at 11:00 a.m. on the sixteenth. He took one look at the rolling hills, the green grass and the bloom on the mares and foals in the fields, and he was sold. By 11:00 p.m., the deal was done. He was forty-nine years old.

He called his wife, Nancy, and told her to pack up—they were moving to Florida. When Campbell formed a seven-person syndicate to buy Dickey Stables for $700,000, it included Joe and his brother, Tom. Besides the Campbells, the rest of the syndicate included William Veeneman, chairman of the board of Churchill Downs, where the Kentucky Derby is run; Thomas Woods, a Cincinnati insurance man and sportsman; and John Hampshire, a Maryland horseman. While the fluctuating ownership of this farm could be a story by itself, over the years O'Farrell was the one constant owner.

The latest in a line of characters who launched the Thoroughbred industry in central Florida, Joe was a smooth-talking hustler, a mover and a shaker who never sat still. Many interviewees said that he was the only man who could get from Ocala to Miami in three to three and a half hours—as long as his license wasn't expired because of too many driving tickets. Brusque and impatient, arrogant and completely certain of his own goals, he was also charismatic and charming. "Too many to count," would be the answer to the question of how many people Joe talked into buying a farm/horse/share/season/partnership. But no matter how much he badgered, bullied and convinced, no one could ever accuse him of not putting his own money, heart and soul into the industry.

Joe was born in 1912 in Westminster, Maryland. He and his brother, Tom, were fascinated with horses from an early age. In 1936, after graduating from Washington University and dabbling in a few business ventures, he and Tom scraped together enough to buy their first mare for $125 and bred her to a stallion by Man o' War. They were on their way, working other jobs while gradually amassing a broodmare band. In 1950, they snagged an unproven sire by the name of Rough'n Tumble. He had beautiful conformation and "the look of eagles," as Tom once said.

"Rough" was a Kentucky-bred that became the first stakes winner and best offspring for his sire, Free For All. Although his sire had been an early

Rough'n Tumble, "the look of eagles." *Photo by Jim Jernigan.*

Kentucky Derby contender, he broke down while finishing fourth in the Derby Trial, unbeaten in his previous six starts. Although he retired to a decent stud in Kentucky, he never foaled anything that would amount to much except Rough'n Tumble. Rough's dam, Roused, was a non-winner and bore no other stars but was by the great Bull Dog. Harold and Frances Genter purchased the small bay colt privately. He raced well at two, winning a stakes in his second start and showing talent subsequently, but he was knocked out of the classics by a splint. When he won the Santa Anita Derby in 1951, O'Farrell noticed. Unfortunately, the recurring splint prevented the talented horse from entering the Kentucky Derby. Since he continued to have a problem leg, the Genters agreed with their trainer, Sunshine Calvert, that he should be retired.

Despite the talent he had exhibited, Kentucky did not want him, which later proved to be a stroke of luck for Florida. In his racing career, he exhibited both speed and stamina, qualities highly coveted by the growing herd of Florida breeders. The O'Farrell brothers purchased an interest in him and brought him to Maryland to stand. That first year, they asked $250 but took less if the owner couldn't pay it. Thus, he was part of the O'Farrell holdings at the time they started up in Florida.

The original Dickey Stables was two pieces of land that the new syndicate united by buying another piece from Rosemere, raising the total to eight hundred acres. Included in that original purchase were all twenty-one head of Leach's stock, including Noodle Soup, who was about to become the most famous broodmare in the United States. The syndicate began shipping in its own stock, as well as purchasing new. Soon there were some sixty mares on the farm and four stallions—King's Stride, Bull Brier, Fly Away and, for one quick season, Rough'n Tumble.

The training barns also filled up. Roy Yates, who had trained Needles when it was still Dickey Leach Farm, managed one barn. Colonel Randolph Tayloe, another Marylander and a retired army officer, managed another. Eventually, all the barns would be named for famous horses raised and trained at Ocala Stud: Needles, Leather Button, Wayward Bird, King Hairan; Noodle Soup was the broodmare barn.

From the start, it was O'Farrell who ran the show. He immediately brought in Karl Koontz from Maryland to be the business manager and publicity director. A past editor of *Chronicle of the Horse* in Maryland, Koontz took his job seriously, and Ocala Stud became one of the most publicized farms in the country. He remembers well his ride with Joe down from Maryland to see the wilds of Marion County the first time. "Joe was so enthusiastically pointing out all the sights as we drove along old Highway 301, telling me to look at those big oaks, the horses and the grass, that he'd forgotten to gas up and we ran out!"

In a mid-1980s interview, Bonnie Heath remembered that in those days, there were six of them trying to make the Thoroughbred industry go: Carl Rose, Doug Stewart of Shady Lane Farm, George Cavanaugh of Pinecrest Farm, Grant Dorland of Roseland Farm, Joe and him. Whether the problem

Ocala Stud in 1967. *Photo by Jim Jernigan.*

Ocala Stud. *Courtesy Florida State News Bureau.*

was political, equine or agricultural, they'd all get together to solve it. But of them all, Joe was the eternal optimist, his enthusiasm for Marion County as a place to raise and train horses unlimited. He went to horse sales all over the country. The minute someone bought a horse, he was at their elbow, trying to talk them into sending it to Florida to train. Many of them caved in to his insistent persuasion. Like Rose before him, O'Farrell spent hundreds of hours and days helping newcomers find and set up their farms.

"He was opinionated, stubborn, obstinate, but he was also kind-hearted and unselfish," Koontz would say of him years later. He added that Joe also gave away free advice and free services to his stallions; he'd rush to help anybody with an equine emergency no matter the time of night or day. He never took a salary when he later ran *The Florida Horse* or the Florida Breeders' Sales Company.

Author and friend Chuck Tilley said, "He hit the ground running, and he never stopped. The first time I ever saw him was at the Keeneland sales in his big, old, broad-brimmed hat and shirtsleeves [at a time when people used to dress up at the sales]. He would talk to anyone that stopped long enough to listen, trying to get people to send their horses to Florida to train. And a lot of them did!"

Son Michael O'Farrell remembered many times sitting with new arrivals in the clubhouse at the top of a hill where the Paddock Mall now sits. Joe would put them up, wine and dine them and make sure that they found farms before they left town. Some didn't appreciate his badgering, and more than one met the force of his blunt and sometimes abrasive attitude. But many came.

Joe invited Chuck Tilley to come down to Florida and look the place over in 1961. Tilley remembered sitting in the clubhouse while various horsemen came in to talk to him. Every once in a while, Joe would stick his head in and say, "'Come on, let's go look at farms.' I thought there'd be a bunch of

Joe holding a press conference in front of the clubhouse. *Courtesy* The Florida Horse.

Joe O'Farrell doing his thing in 1963: talking someone into something. *Photo by Jim Jernigan.*

them. Well, he was a very fast driver, what I'd call a reckless driver. Those were mostly dirt roads back then, no main roads or I-75. And he always smoked these big cigars, so the smoke would be boiling inside the car. He'd go wheeling around on those roads and circle a farm, and I couldn't see anything for the smoke and dust! He'd say, 'Here's this one' and 'There's that one.' Some of them I never found again. I still wonder if they even existed!"

No one doubted his constant hard work or his dedication to the industry. He was neither modest nor shy, and he didn't hesitate to tell folks what he'd done over the years to promote the industry. He worked even more closely than Rose had with the University of Florida and outside consultants to improve feed. He read about researchers studying Napoleon's hair so he had lab analysts do the same thing with the hair of horses to figure out what was missing in their diet and how to improve nutrition. According to an article by Peter Chew in the *Orlando Sentinel* dated October 10, 1965, he spent $20,000 a year on soil, grass, blood and hair tests of his animals, feeding the data to a large computer at the Martin Company's missile plant in Orlando. The nutritional content of the feed was altered occasionally according to the results of those tests. Gradually, the feed for Marion County horses improved to what is today, a highly scientific blend that ensures equines have what they need.

He was a walking billboard; he may have bought and sold more farms over the years than anyone. He was one of the first to actually borrow money from a bank to buy a horse; it soon became a commonplace idea for banks to own horses. Dick Chazal of Chazal Insurance in Ocala was the first insurance company in the country to insure horses; it was doubtless Joe who talked him into it.

Florida was beginning to have an influx of decent bloodlines. Heath brought in better-quality stallions: Curandero from the King Ranch and Preakness winner Alsab, and of course, Needles came home to stand. Meanwhile, turning the coin over, King Hairan became the first good Florida-bred to retire to Kentucky, increasing the prestige of Florida-breds. By 1958, few were arguing the fact that Florida-breds could run, especially the precocious 2-year-olds. Several stallions standing in Florida had made decent names for themselves—*Samurai, Ariel Game, Noble Hero and King's Stride among them. But one of the great things O'Farrell did for

Rough'n Tumble at Ocala Stud. *Painting by Angie Draper.*

Florida was bring the stallion Rough'n Tumble down from Maryland for that first season. Florida was about to get its first real foundation sire. This beautifully conformed horse eventually established a Florida bloodline.

Rough's first small crop arrived in 1955. After standing the 1956 season in Florida, he was shipped back to Maryland for the 1957 season. By then, his first Maryland-bred progeny were running well, exciting the breeders in Marion County. With that first small crop at the races, he stood eleventh on the stallion lists nationwide. Ocala Stud soon purchased him outright. The Genters agreed to let him go with one stipulation: they would get the pick of his 1957 crop. By the end of 1957, he was the leading 2-year-old sire in the nation.

In January 1957, the first full crop of foals under the Ocala Stud management hit the ground. They hit the tracks in 1959, and by the end of that year, they boasted 12 winners of twenty-seven races, earning Ocala Stud the reputation of being one of the best juvenile breeders in the nation. By August, counting boarders as well as horses bred by the farm, those figures had risen to 104 winners and 11 stakes-placed winners. This was an incredible start by anyone's standards.

Although by the end of 1959, Carl Rose was once again the leading breeder for the state with thirty-eight winners—Ocala Stud was second with twenty-nine but led by earnings—it would be Rose's last time to lead. With only two crops to race, the new farm in town had already earned $436,985, more than established Kentucky breeders like Leslie Combs II, Elmendorf Farm, Maine Chance Farm, Fred Hooper and many more. Reporters began calling Ocala Stud the "General Motors of Thoroughbred Breeding." By 1960, Rough'n Tumble was leading the nation's juvenile sires list, and Ocala Stud was tenth on the national breeders' lists with fifty-six winners and $655,075 in total earnings. In its first three years of business, Ocala Stud bred or sold winners of more than $1 million. It was the leading commercial breeder in the nation, if one of the first, since the idea of commercial breeding was just taking hold.

Joe O'Farrell's participation changed nearly everything in the industry. As winter racing became more and more popular, and Florida-breds appeared to mature earlier than those raised in cold, winter barns, Florida tracks began holding earlier and earlier juvenile races. While some traditional breeders were appalled at pushing a young horse so, the young FTBA endorsed the idea, and its 2-year-olds were soon proving themselves before anyone else's had even hit the tracks.

Joe had a hand in this beginning with that first crop when it came of age in 1957. From that day to this, the farm has sold its entire juvenile crop, feeling that this best assures the buyer that it is not holding back its best. Joe liked Rose's idea of selling ready-made racehorses the minute they were old enough to show their stuff, but he thought he could do one better. He, too, recognized that the pedigrees did not yet compete with other states like Kentucky, New York and Maryland. Performance was the best way to sell a Florida-bred, and the best timing was as juveniles, while northern-breds were still catching up in growth. The advantage of such a method was immediately obvious. Buyers did not have to wonder if their yearling would measure up to its pedigree or pay the expense of both dollars and the angst of getting a young horse through its initial training without injury. The buyer could take a horse straight out of such a sale and immediately put it to work earning back its purchase price.

At a time when most of the national breeding industry raised its horses to sell as yearlings or raced its own stock, O'Farrell decided to create a new kind of sale. He took his first batch of 2-year-olds to Hialeah and talked the established auction house, Fasig-Tipton, into conducting a sale on February 27, 1957. They galloped the horses before the sale so everyone could see them under tack. Even Joe's usual bravado quailed when he later realized what he had done. As he said in an interview with *Sports Illustrated* on January 23, 1967, "There I was in the Hialeah paddock with 26 2-year-olds bred like billy goats! And just as that sale started, it began to rain. I'd put every cent I had into that sale. If a hard rain chased away the buyers, I figured I would be bankrupt before I even got going." Though modest, it was a success.

O'Farrell immediately planned the next sale but ran into a snag. Hialeah would not allow another sale of what looked like a private Ocala Stud stock sale, fearing that every breeder would want to hold its own sale at the track. That really was O'Farrell's intention, but now he had to regroup.

So O'Farrell, Rose, Heath and Stewart created the Florida Breeders' Sales Association. They were quickly joined by Grant Dorland, George Cavanaugh and Bruce Campbell. They held their new company's first sale at the Hialeah Municipal Auditorium in 1958. The annual Baby Show was incorporated as part of the sales. While rain was a factor in the not-so-waterproof building, the sale was again a success. By now, the first graduates from the year before had emerged as good racehorses, so the idea was proven sound.

Bruce Campbell told Chuck Tilley in an article written in the *Daily Racing Form* in 1974, "The wind was picking up sand and throwing it at horses and humans like little bullets. I think if a man stuck his hand up to bid, he got burned by the sand. Come to think of it maybe that's why there wasn't much bidding."

Humphrey Finney of Fasig-Tipton, which would continue to be the company's auctioneers for twenty-five years, said, "A cold west wind had the horses on their toes and what a sale it was…From that day to this, Florida has been the best spot in the U.S.A. to hold a sale of race horses. The reason is obvious. Only in Florida does one find in one area the stables from New England, New York, New Jersey, Maryland, Michigan and Chicago. If you have a good horse to offer, you'll have a buyer."

Thirty-seven head sold on this auspicious night, twenty-six of them admittedly still Ocala Stud stock. One was a half-sister to Needles, but the sales topper was a $15,200 colt that would go on to become a stakes winner, Four Fives. When another sold for $12,000, and the overall average was a respectable $5,200, the new company was ecstatic. It was clear that O'Farrell had created a new method of marketing Florida-breds—a new method of marketing horses. This first formal sales crop also ran off to prove itself.

Since Hialeah still wouldn't allow use of its pavilion, the next sale was held in a machine shed, with a candy-striped tent to cover the audience. George Cavanaugh would later say, "We didn't make any money, but we sure had fun, getting out there in the morning and breezing the 2-year-olds. We'd match them with anybody who had one ready to go."

The early years continued a bit rough, with the tent flooding one year and lights going out another year, with horses and people panicking and running for the exits. Yet the invention of 2-year-old sales was one of the most effective tools ever produced to promote the Florida industry, and it changed the industry nationwide. By 1960, fifty-six youngsters had gone through the Florida Breeders' Sales Association sales. By fall, fifty-one were starters, with seventy races won and average earnings of $8,121, well above the national average of $2,493.

Sales facilities were constructed at Tropical, the Doyle Conner pavilion in Ocala, and a new sales pavilion was finally erected by Hialeah; stabling at all three of the southern racetracks supported the sales. By 1962, two sessions were required to handle the numbers of horses rolling in; it became three sessions by 1964.

By mid-November 1963, ninety of the ninety-six horses sold that year had already started in major competition. In the Garden State Stakes, one of the nation's blue-ribbon races for 2-year-olds, four of the fourteen starters had been sold in the FBSC sale. The four, purchased for a total of $63,000, had earned more than $450,000. The sales had proven themselves.

The company incorporated, changing its name to Florida Breeders' Sales Company. At its first meeting on October 6, 1963, at the Ocala Stud

Inside the Hialeah Sales pavilion. *Courtesy Coady Photography/Hialeah archives.*

clubhouse, O'Farrell was made the first president, Cavanaugh the vice-president and Stewart the secretary, while Heath, Campbell and Dorland were made board members.

At the next meeting, on November 25, it was moved that members' horses be sold the first two nights of the sale. Each member was allotted a one-sixth share of the forty-four available Hialeah stalls, but ultimately, it still favored Ocala Stud, which got thirteen stalls; D&H Stable, nine; Pinecrest Farm, nine; Shady Lane Farm, nine; Roseland Farm, three; and Bruce Campbell, two. A partnership with Fasig-Tipton was proposed by John Finney, and on December 1, 1964, it was completed.

It was still the only 2-year-old sale in the country. But there was now a selection process involved, so Fasig-Tipton decided to conduct its own 2-year-old sale, picking up the discards of FBSC following the select sales.

October 12, 1962, was the day that the FBSC held its first mixed auction (mostly breeding stock but no age restriction), under a tent at Ocala Stud. A tour of the farm had been held the day before. The second FBSC sale in Ocala, in 1963, included the "FTBA Ocala Weekend,"

Breezing the sales horses in October 1964. *Photo by Jim Jernigan.*

complete with two dinners sponsored by FTBA and the Farm Managers' Club. Eventually, this would grow into "Ocala Week," a weeklong series of tours, events and the big sale of broodmares and breeding stock that still goes on in October today. By 1966, the FTBA had moved its annual elections to the same week, and the annual Stallion Parade was created. The Fillies' Follies, a group of equine industry women, performed an annual skit to raise money for charity, and this became another stock feature of the week.

Soon the pattern was three annual sales consisting of the Hialeah sale of Florida-bred 2-year-olds in training, held in January during the racing meet; the Sunshine Park (Tampa) sales for horses of all ages, held in March; and the Ocala sale of horses of all ages, held in October. The increasingly popular 2-year-old sales were quickly dubbed the "Sale Where the Buyer Gets the Break."

By January 1968, the 2-year-old sales had become so popular that new stabling was provided at both Hialeah and Gulfstream just to house the sales horses while in session. Walkways were built as protection against downpours, and best of all, the newly expanded sales pavilion boasted a new, revolving

Early pioneers. *From left to right*: Roy Yates, Bruce Campbell, Joe O'Farrell, Eugene Mori, Doug Donn, Bonnie Heath, Elmer Heubeck and Carl Rose. *Photo by Jim Jernigan.*

auctioneer's stand in the pavilion. The horses became a more select group, and more stringent veterinary inspections were required.

In 1976, Tilley wrote, "No sale in the country sent out such a high percentage of winners as did the Hialeah sales of Florida-bred, 2-year-olds in training. In the beginning they didn't sell for a lot of money, but there was an advantage there too. Trainers bought them for their own accounts, and you don't sell many bad racing prospects to trainers spending their own money." Ocala Stud continues the tradition today. Champion Musical Romance was a $22,000 purchase through the April sales in 2009.

The period from 1958 through the early 1960s was a heady time for Florida breeders and their new industry. Everything they touched seemed to turn to gold. In 1958, the same year of the first FBSC sale, the breeders created *The Florida Horse* magazine. *Florida Thoroughbred* had already been claimed by a bloodstock agency in Miami putting out its own little magazine, and although that only lasted for two issues, the FTBA was forced instead to adopt the name *The Florida Horse*. The first few issues were produced in the barn where Needles was born, appropriately enough. The magazine's stated purpose was to promote the FBSC sales.

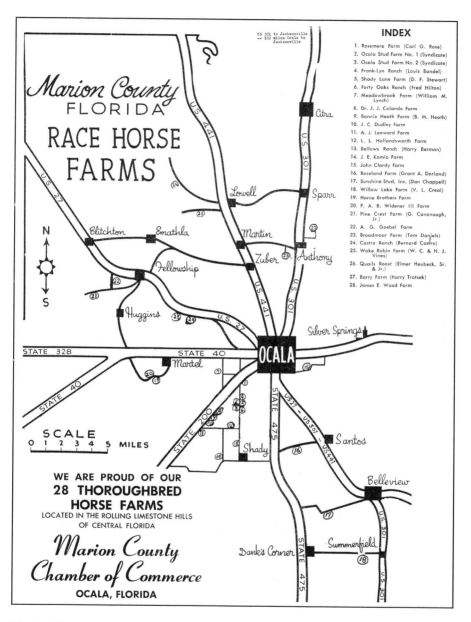

INDEX

1. Rosemere Farm (Carl G. Rose)
2. Ocala Stud Farm No. 1 (Syndicate)
3. Ocala Stud Farm No. 2 (Syndicate)
4. Frank-Lyn Ranch (Louis Bandel)
5. Shady Lane Farm (D. F. Stewart)
6. Forty Oaks Ranch (Fred Hilton)
7. Meadowbrook Farm (William M. Lynch)
8. Dr. J. J. Colando Farm
9. Bonnie Heath Farm (B. M. Heath)
10. J. C. Dudley Farm
11. A. J. Leeward Farm
12. L. L. Hollandsworth Farm
13. Bellows Ranch (Harry Berman)
14. J. E. Komlo Farm
15. John Clardy Farm
16. Roseland Farm (Grant A. Dorland)
17. Sunshine Stud, Inc. (Dan Chappell)
18. Willow Lake Farm (V. L. Creal)
19. Horne Brothers Farm
20. P. A. B. Widener III Farm
21. Pine Crest Farm (G. Cavanaugh, Jr.)
22. A. G. Goebel Farm
23. Broadmoor Farm (Tom Daniels)
24. Castro Ranch (Bernard Castro)
25. Wake Robin Farm (W. C. & H. J. Vines)
26. Quails Roost (Elmer Heubeck, Sr. & Jr.)
27. Barry Farm (Harry Trotsek)
28. James E. Wood Farm

WE ARE PROUD OF OUR
28 THOROUGHBRED HORSE FARMS
LOCATED IN THE ROLLING LIMESTONE HILLS
OF CENTRAL FLORIDA

Marion County Chamber of Commerce
OCALA, FLORIDA

Map in *The Florida Horse* in October 1958. *Courtesy* The Florida Horse.

The first issue came out in June 1958. Karl Koontz, already putting out a newsletter for Ocala Stud in which he reported new foals, stallion crops and other news, was made the first editor, while Chuck Tilley would follow

Karl Koontz. *Photo by Charlene R. Johnson.*

Chuck Tilley producing *Farm Directory*. *Photo by Art Kunkel.*

in his wake. The Mackle brothers' Elkcam Stable's Hubcap was featured on that first cover winning the Swift Handicap. Inside this magazine was a map showing all the farms in the county, twenty-eight now.

This first issue was followed in October with the first *Florida Horse Stallion Register*, featuring fifty-nine stallions. This special edition of *The Florida Horse* continues to come out every year at the time mare owners are choosing stallions for the following spring matches.

In 1960, after Heath was elected president, the FTBA meetings were held more and more in the Ocala area. The first meeting place was in the same tack room of the old barn where Needles had been born, followed by a stone building that housed a barbecue, where they began meeting three times per year. The shift had formally been made from south to central Florida.

Chapter 5

THE OCALA ERA

It was time for the Genters to make their choice. Harold and Frances Genter and their trainer, Sunshine Calvert, had inspected the 1957 foal crop by Rough'n Tumble several times. Joe O'Farrell, who knew well what ran out in his paddocks, was banking on the fact that the Genters had always raced colts. They had narrowed the field to two colts and a filly out of Iltis. The tiebreaker finally occurred when they realized that the filly had been born on Mrs. Genter's birthday, February 17. Although Harold Genter was in favor, he still considered it a sentimental decision, so they named the filly My Dear Girl, which he often called his wife. Sentiments or no, it was clear that the three knew their horses—both colts and the filly would become stakes horses.

Meanwhile, Rough'n Tumble was well on the road to making a name for himself. One of his fillies, Wedlock, a $4,500 purchase through the sales, became the first Florida-bred female to win a classic when she won the Kentucky Oaks in 1959. In fact, Florida-breds captured 40 percent of the purses in this distaff Kentucky classic. Running fourth behind Wedlock was New Star by *Stella Aurata, which stood at Shady Lane, while Indian Maid by Rinaldo placed second in the split division of the same race.

At first, My Dear Girl wasn't so dear when she refused good gate manners. In the hands of a different trainer, since Calvert was already north with the Genters' main string, she was so unruly in the gate that she broke badly in her first start and never caught up to the field. In her second start, the Florida Breeders' Stakes, she broke through the stall, banging her jockey's

Iltis and My Dear Girl. *Painting by Angie Draper.*

My Dear Girl wins the Florida Breeders Stakes in 1959. *Photo by Jerry and Leo Frutkoff.*

head on the top of the gate. Once reloaded, however, she led the charge of twenty-five 2-year-olds the three-furlong distance to win by two lengths as a 179-5 longshot. Never again would she be a longshot.

She shipped north to Calvert, who patiently took the time to retrain her to the gate, plying her with sugar and standing in the stalls with her for hours. While she continued to show that she had a mind of her own, the gate was never again a problem. She won her next start, the Miss Chicago Stakes, while setting a track record, and she placed in a second stakes with sore shins.

Indeed, the filly was a sentimental proposition; she quickly became a favorite for the Genters and everyone else. "My Dear Girl was the first filly we ever raced," Mrs. Genter said in a later interview. "She always had a special place in my heart, but she definitely had a mind of her own. She always wanted her own way. Yet, I could walk into her stall, feed her carrots or sugar and she was as gentle and calm as could be. I fell completely in love with her."

Mrs. Frances Genter in 1983. *Photo by Charlene R. Johnson.*

The year 1959 was a great one for Florida breeders. As King Hairan had run in the shadow of Needles, so now did Indian Maid, the best Florida-bred 2-year-old of 1958, race in the shadow of My Dear Girl. Indian Maid had already run the fastest mile of any filly or mare in the history of Churchill Downs and shared the honor of the fastest filly or mare in the United States. She would eventually accumulate more than $200,000 in earnings, a remarkable sum for a Florida-bred *and* for a filly of those times. Although she still would not be the best of this year, she, along with several other talented horses, added to the growing glamour of the upstart Florida-breds stealing Kentucky's trophies.

My Dear Girl was named Champion 2-Year-Old, with earnings of $185,622. No one could dispute this champion's Florida-bred status, having been conceived as well as dropped in the Sunshine State. Exuberant Marion

County breeders had a champion, a top handicap mare, and Florida-breds had won or placed in thirty-four open stakes races. Rough'n Tumble was fourth on the nation's leading sire list of juvenile winners. His stud fee shot from $250 to $1,000 in 1959 and then to $5,000 in 1960, far surpassing any other stallion in the state. By 1961, turf writers were speculating that Rough'n Tumble was the greatest horse ever to stand in Maryland, ranking him above Native Dancer and Discovery—and he only stood two seasons there!

Rough also proved to be a top broodmare sire. My Dear Girl helped that record along by becoming as strong a foundation mare as Rough was stallion. She produced thirteen winners from fifteen foals, eight stakes horses and four stakes producers.

Rough'n Tumble still did not have access to the quality of mares Kentucky, Maryland and New York breeders had, and so his production of consistently fast and talented racehorses counted for even more than other stallions. By the time he died at Ocala Stud in 1968, he commanded a stud fee of $20,000, and his 2-year-olds sold as high as $70,000. By 1968, his progeny had earned more than $5 million, and he was a sire of champions. He had blatantly set his stamp to Florida-breds that would carry through many generations to come. His male line would continue to be responsible for champions and champion sires: Holy Bull, Montbrook, High Cotton, Trippi and Notebook among many. He was also about to produce a horse that would earn more accolades than any other horse in history, still to modern day. Florida finally had its own bloodline, not passed down for generations dating back to Europe but rather proven in the racing wars, over and over so that none could doubt its validity.

Rough's breeding career was cut short by sore feet from past foundering, which prevented him from being a comfortable breeder. In November 1967, Ocala Stud cut the ribbon on its new equine swimming pool, sixty feet in diameter and thirteen feet deep. While rare, and the first in Florida, the local paper acknowledged that California had been swimming horses for some time. This one was built for the "Old Man," as twenty-year-old Rough'n Tumble was called. His health was declining, and they hoped to ease the pain in his legs.

He was retired from the breeding shed in 1968; by April, he was put down. He was Florida's leading sire for more than a decade and one of only a few sires anywhere at the time to sire winners of more than $4 million. He was buried at Ocala Stud, where they created a new equine cemetery for him. Rough'n Tumble, along with Joe O'Farrell and Ocala Stud, had changed the face of Florida and the Thoroughbred industry forever.

Ocala Stud Swimming Pool in January 1968. *Photo by Jim Jernigan.*

Downtown Ocala, 1959. *Photo by Jim Jernigan.*

The state and the county were enthusiastically behind this blossoming industry. The chamber of commerce consistently advertised the beauty of the farms. In 1959, the Department of Agriculture produced a sixty-page booklet depicting Thoroughbred racing and breeding in the state. When Farris Bryant became governor in 1960 in support of the industry, the last hurdle was jumped when, pushed by the FTBA, he finally passed the breeders' bill, State Senate Bill #601, which implemented a preferred program—one race per day written at each track allowing Florida-breds first choice as entries, and with some $460,000 to be distributed to the breeders of winning Florida-breds. The breeders didn't want closed races, just an opportunity to run. So good was the program at promoting the state's breeding program that both Maryland and Illinois sought Florida's help in establishing similar bills of their own.

As the industry began to explode in Marion County, it died out in south Florida. The Christophers sold off farm and horses, and Charlie O'Neil died. A few new farms that were started in the south were short-lived. The "Kingdom of the Sun" was off and running, with new equine interests arriving every day. In five short years, the four farms of Needles's time had blossomed into forty-six, with a combined value of more than $15 million. From 75 foals registered in Needles' year of 1953, there were now 350. More brave Kentuckians joined the ranks. Harry Isaacs, one of the most successful breeders in the country and famous for his horses' names all starting with the letter *I*, purchased 650 acres and combined his Maryland and Kentucky operations into one Florida farm, named Brookfield Farm. Former ambassador John Hay Whitney and his sister, Mrs. Charles Shipman Payson, built a Marion County annex for their famous Greentree Stud Farms, three hundred acres of grassland directly across the road from Ocala Stud.

Mrs. Elizabeth Whitney Tippett built an Ocala branch of her famous Kentucky-based Llangollen Farm, and B.A. Dario transferred his breeding operation from Rhode Island to Ocala. Robert Marks, in Ocala since 1951, purchased 509 acres for fifty dollars per acre. In 1961, he started Robin's Nest Farm, where he stood such popular stallions as Ridan and *Noholme II, one of his greatest contributions to Marion County. Both *Noholme II and his son Nodouble would be leading Florida sires for many years, with *Noholme II leading the nation in 1969 and Nodouble in 1981. As of 2014, that farm is Kinsman Stud.

In 1958, Meadowbrook Farm was created from a 172-acre farm off of Highway 200. William M. Lynch built beautiful new barns and track and shipped his horses to John Nerud, a trainer in Hollywood, California. But within a year, Lynch gave up the farm to a new syndicate headed by C.H. Lovely. An active member in the syndicate was Joseph LaCroix and his wife, Barbara, who would become major figures in the Thoroughbred scene of Marion County for many years and, ultimately, sole owners of Meadowbrook Farm. Under this new ownership, high-quality broodmares entered the county, and the farm grew to some 400 acres.

But while the industry soared, other breeders still refused to be impressed. Whitney Tower wrote in *Sports Illustrated* on October 2, 1961, that while Florida-breds earned $2,620,717 in 1960, just one Kentucky farm, Calumet, earned more than $3 million. It was time for the next champion.

ANOTHER HUSTLER CAME to town. Jack Price, creator of the Winslow Manufacturing Company, a machine-tool company, started out as a young Western Union messenger around the Ohio tracks, running books as a sideline. A young newsstand clerk named Katherine Boyle was one of his steadiest customers. A former "Harvey Girl," she had loved horses as long as Jack had; they married in 1931. While always dabbling in horses, Jack expanded his successful company and then sold it to his brothers.

On the profits of the sale in the early 1950s, Jack and Katherine finally indulged their passion for horses. They created Dorchester Farm outside Cleveland, Ohio, and then in 1956 decided to ship their youngsters south to Ocala Stud to be broken and trained. When two stakes horses were the result, the Prices moved to Coral Gables so Jack could train in the sunshine. On their way south to Ocala Stud, their three mares, including a $300 mare named Joppy, were bred to a Maryland stallion named Saggy.

By Saggy out of Joppy, a brown colt was born at Ocala Stud on April 16, 1958, and named for a tax loophole, Carry Back. The tiny colt never grew to be very big, disappointing owner and farm managers alike. Yet by the time he was a yearling, he was already showing aggressive determination. While he would never weigh even one thousand pounds, the little brown horse with the long tail would win the hearts of an enchanted public.

Not expecting much out of him, Price dropped the youngster into races as an early 2-year-old—very early. His first race was January 29, 1960, and he wasn't even two years old yet. He started that first year by showing flashes of brilliance amid mediocre racing. He reduced one track record for five furlongs by a full second, an astonishing feat. He showed enough to justify his owner/trainer in sending him to New York, where he proceeded to win several major stakes races, including the world's richest race, the

Joppy and Carry Back. *Painting by Angie Draper.*

Garden State Stakes. Unbelievably, he ended his first year with total earnings of $286,299, the leading money-winning 2-year-old in Florida history. His fans dubbed him the "colt from the wrong side of the tracks" for his colorful—though not very blue—bloodlines.

Fred Hooper, not yet a Florida breeder, had a classics hopeful of his own, Crozier. Crozier and Carry Back met for the first time in their 3-year-old year in the Everglades Handicap. For the rest of the year, these two provided the thrilling duels that racing legends are made of. Like Needles, Carry Back had a come-from-behind style that left his fans' hearts in their throats. Unlike Needles, he was tiny, so it never looked possible that he could get the job done. This race set the pattern: Crozier would leap out, charging for the lead, while Carry Back would trail far behind. Then, as if sprouting wings, he would fly, catching the much larger horse just in time to thrust his neck or head or nose ahead at the line. So grueling were the duels between these two that some of the other horses that dared enter the ring with them broke down in their wake. The people loved Carry Back. Turf writers dubbed him the "People's Choice," the epitome of a Cinderfella, rags-to-riches story.

Carry Back winning the Kentucky Derby. *Courtesy* The Florida Horse.

His racing style might have been similar, but Carry Back was not at all like placid Needles in temperament. The charismatic horse could not stand still; fidgeting and biting were his favorite pastimes. His grooms usually ended up as wet as he after a bath—and often with bruises.

Neither Price nor his wife ever expected to be the owners of such a character or the stars of such a show. Katherine personally kept up with all the fan mail, often referring to Carry Back as though he were a person. In later years, she would refer to him as "my son, the stallion." They were swept up by and into the racing scene, and they loved it.

By Kentucky Derby time, Carry Back was the firm favorite. A special train carried 175 people from Marion County to Lexington to view the famous race. The race caller of the day, Bryan Field, would never be allowed to forget his famous words early in the race, "Carry Back is too far back to make it!"

Fred Hooper had been trying to reclaim the Derby trophy ever since Hoop Jr. Crozier was his greatest hope yet, but the small brown horse with the long tail from the wrong side of the tracks would dash his dream once more. Coming from even farther behind than Needles had, Carry Back seemed to cover twice the ground, stride for stride, as the other horses.

Joe with friends under the bell. *Courtesy* The Florida Horse.

Michael O'Farrell, second generation, under the bell in 2013. *Photo by Charlene R. Johnson.*

With all the grit of his great heart, he pulled ahead of Crozier and the others by what was, for him, a phenomenal three-quarters of a length.

Just the day before, a great brass bell, taken off the decommissioned USS *Kentucky*, had been hung from a tower at Ocala Stud to swing over a symbolic chunk of limerock. The bell is still there, despite many efforts on the part of Kentuckians to buy it, but it is no longer rung. "It's so loud," Mike O'Farrell said in 2013. "Everyone in the mall and the college could hear it if we rang it. It'd probably cause traffic accidents."

But in 1961, the moment Carry Back crossed the finish line, Nancy O'Farrell raced out and began ringing the bell, proclaiming for all who could hear that Florida was two for two in the Kentucky Derby. For the rest of his life, Fred Hooper would mourn both the money he might have made and the coveted Derby win he might have had had Carry Back just been born a different year.

For the second year in a row, Florida-breds exceeded the $2 million mark. As with Needles, Carry Back also prompted a surge in the growth of Thoroughbred farms in Marion and surrounding counties. Almost immediately, six new farms sprouted in Marion County.

Carry Back went on to capture the second leg of the Triple Crown, the Preakness, the first Florida-bred to capture that prestigious Maryland race. Up to that point, only Kentucky, Maryland and Virginia had ever produced a winner of that race. Turf writer Joe Kolb of the *Fort Lauderdale News* wrote that "in the final quarter mile, Carry Back appears to be assisted by a jet."

Carry Back is given the key to the city. *Courtesy* The Florida Horse.

In June 1961, columnist Bud Wallace of the *Lexington Herald* wailed that Ocala Stud was getting too close to the top of the nation's breeding list, an honor that none but a Kentucky farm had ever earned. In defense, the Kentucky Thoroughbred Breeders' Association was formed to promote the Kentucky industry. Other turf writers noted the speed of the phenomenal growth of the industry in Marion County, surpassing anywhere, including California. Carry Back was given the key to the city of Ocala and honorary membership to the chamber of commerce.

Ocala loved its equine stars, so much so that in September 1961, when plans for a major highway named I-75 to cut through horse country were made known, they were met with a concerted effort by the FTBA and the local politicians to reroute it. The federal plan to connect all major cities with six-lane highways had already cut through Kentucky horse country; Florida breeders intended to prevent the same fate. An early proposal was to send it down Shady Road, which was met with unanimous opposition. Shady Road fronted Ocala Stud, Greentree Farm, Shady Lane Farm, Rosemere Stud, Forty Oaks Ranch and many others. They requested it be rerouted three miles west. The highway was rerouted. Of course, today horse country is now on the *other* side of I-75, and only a few farms remain along Shady Road.

Florida was not to gain its first Triple Crown winner just yet. Carry Back injured an ankle in the Belmont and finished a disappointing seventh. Before his 4-year-old year, Price proudly took credentials in hand to offer Carry Back to some of the finest Kentucky farms as a stud. He was rejected.

As a 4-year-old, Carry Back always finished in the money, although it took a while to gain a win again. But when he defeated two-time Horse of the Year Kelso and equaled the track record in the Metropolitan, he became Florida's first millionaire. He stood behind only Round Table, Nashua and Citation for the most earnings of any racehorse ever.

Now Kentuckians made a bid for the little horse. Instead, Price retired Carry Back to Ocala Stud at the end of his 4-year-old season, where he serviced thirty mares in 1963. Joe O'Farrell stated that in twenty-five years, he'd never seen a horse do what Carry Back had done and still be as sound as he was. But Price was not through yet. He kept the stallion in light training and, after that breeding season, sent him back to the races.

Carry Back would finally retire for good with $1,241,165 and a record of sixty-one starts—a number few racehorses today ever near—with twenty-one wins, eleven seconds and eleven thirds. This time, he did go to Kentucky. But in 1968, after standing four years in the Bluegrass State, he returned home to Dorchester. There he was treated to Jell-O mix and Life Savers by his doting "parents."

Jack used his phenomenal winnings to build Dorchester Equine Preparatory Academy in Marion County. A sign at the entrance read, "The Farm that Carry Back Built." This was something new, a "school" for both young horses and young boys aspiring to become exercise riders and jockeys. Dorchester Equine Preparatory School received some forty-five four-legged students its first year in 1964. While some old-timers thought Price was crazy, others deemed it the "world's most modern facility," the first major breakthrough in horse training in two hundred years.

For the first nine months, the weanlings had supervised play while undergoing periodic physical examinations and X-rays. The final three months were devoted to breaking and training under racetrack conditions. Monthly reports were sent to owners. A veterinarian and blacksmith were on duty at all times. Stalls were called dormitories and were equipped with hi-fi units to provide soothing music. They were cleaned with vacuum cleaners. Colts were kept in Carry Back Hall and fillies in Regret Hall. A loudspeaker system acclimated the young horses to the sounds of a track. Tuition fees ran higher than Yale at $3,600 per year. (Human college averaged $2,500.) Regular photographs and recorded daily tapes were made on every horse. On graduation day, the yearlings paraded across a stage to receive diplomas and certificates of health and soundness and to show their "parents" what they had learned.

Years later, Mayor Wayne Rubinas declared April 17, 1983, to be Needles and Carry Back Day. Carry Back did not quite make it to his special day; he died on March 25, 1983, less than a year after Jack sold Dorchester Farm. Two years later, the stallion was laid to rest in a ceremony at Churchill Downs, one of only three Derby winners to receive that honor. Needles, the oldest surviving Kentucky Derby winner at the age of thirty, was given a huge carrot, oat, hay and molasses cake back at his barn. A celebration was held at the Ocala Jockey Club, attended by media, horsemen and politicians. Jockey Eddie Arcaro was there to emcee the two very old film clips of the horses' Derby races. "Carry Back taught us the meaning of gameness," Price said tearfully to the crowd gathered that day.

Needles died on October 15, 1984, quietly and peacefully in his stall. On November 8, the chamber of commerce recognized its deceased member and adopted a resolution acknowledging "the many invaluable contributions and fame which Needles and his owners have brought to Ocala and Marion County." The resolution stated that these contributions were "recognized throughout the nation and the world."

Needles turns thirty, the oldest living Kentucky Derby winner. *Courtesy* The Florida Horse.

In 1963, Chuck Tilley, thirty-six, resigned from the *Thoroughbred Record* to become the editor of *The Florida Horse*, the "publication of the FBSC and the official organ of the FTBA." The magazine would change ownership status a few times during its life; as of 2014, it is firmly owned by the breeders' organization.

Ocala Stud grew to more than one thousand acres and stood 17 stallions that welcomed more than 300 mares for the breeding season, making it second only to Spendthrift Farm in Lexington as the leading stallion station in the nation. In November 1961, Ocala Stud broke 158 yearlings, the largest group in training at a single farm in the entire United States.

O'Farrell claimed to spend some $50,000 per year on advertising. One of his methods, to the delight of his boarders, was to send a small ceramic statuette of a foal—available in five different colors and poses—to every broodmare owner upon birth of the new foal. Around the tiny necks hung a sterling silver map of Florida with the foaling date, color, sex, dam and sire inscribed on it.

Joe O'Farrell had done too good a job. The operation had become so large that some of the syndicate owners wanted out. Ocala Stud went up for sale in 1962 for an impressive $2.5 million. O'Farrell explained to the press that most of his partners were men up in age and were not willing to work as hard as he at this time of life. After a year of fielding prospective buyers and reorganization, with no question that O'Farrell would remain, a new syndicate was formed, with O'Farrell and a few others controlling the larger portion. By the time this was ironed out, it was 1964, and racing was the largest source of tax revenue for the state. After less than thirty years of growing this new industry, Florida ranked third in the nation in production of Thoroughbred foals for the first time, behind only Kentucky and California. It would never be less than third again.

Carl Rose, the father of the Florida Thoroughbred industry, gazed upon his dream come true with great satisfaction. In 1958, he had his first heart attack. Ever attentive to his people, he helped Elmer and Harriet Heubeck find a farm of their own, Quail Roost. He held on until 1961, still promoting his beloved industry with comments to the press and once again accepting an assignment to the state racing commission. He stayed just long enough to enact a few more important legislative laws, insisting that it was high time the state recognize that parimutuels were big business and needed to be run as proper businesses. Then, his health failing, he resigned.

In the spring of 1961, he closed a deal selling all of his breeding stock to a group of Virginia horsemen headed by Tyson Gilpin, treasurer of Fasig-Tipton Company, including a two-year lease on his farm. He added that the farmland was worth far too much to remain a horse farm. (Indeed, today much of it is the Central Florida College and Paddock Mall.) After Heubeck sold the last of that season's 2-year-old crop at Hialeah, he was approached by Jack Dreyfuss of Dreyfuss Mutual Funds (sent to him by Rose) and asked to find a farm for him. Jack Dreyfuss was the man who "invented" the commonplace mutual fund through direct marketing to the public. Hobeau Farm would be the only other farm Heubeck would ever manage besides his own Quail Roost.

Hobeau bred strictly to race and soon stood five stallions. They accumulated a broodmare band of 75 mares. The farm grew to two thousand acres, fifty employees and some 250 horses altogether. They built a dormitory for staff, including one for fifteen young women, mostly from Germany, Holland and England, who came over as professional exercise riders. These "foreign" girls would stay a few years and then go back home, although it was admitted that few staff ever wanted to leave because they were treated so well. A theater for full-length movies on the farm also presented their horses' races when available. Staff received a percentage from any horse that did well in which they had a

Rose at dedication of a new highway at MacClenny, May 23, 1962. *Courtesy Buddy Rose.*

hand. Dreyfuss would run a successful operation until February 2005, when he sold his farm for $12,750,000.

In those early days of 1962, Rose, without a farm or a horse to manage, went to Hobeau every morning at 6:00 a.m. to "help" Heubeck run the new farm. On March 26, 1962, State Road 200, which Carl Rose had originally built, was named Carl Rose Highway. He received the justified accolades of a grateful community on many levels that day. "No citizen has done more for the state," wrote Paul Ferguson in the *Orlando Sentinel*. A concrete marker and bronze plaque were set up directly across the road from where the first Florida-bred had been foaled in Marion County on Rosemere Farm.

On February 26, 1963, Carl Rose died at the age of seventy of a heart attack. He followed Heubeck around Hobeau all morning, went home, sat down in his chair and never woke up. It was a good day to die.

LOUIS WOLFSON WAS a fan of racing long before he bought his first horse in the late 1950s. Raised in Jacksonville, he bought a few hundred acres near

Ocala in 1959 and christened his acreage Harbor View Farm. He was a wealthy financier famous for being a corporate raider, as well as for having campaigned Native Dancer.

His wife Patrice's passion for the sport came naturally, as she was the daughter of Hall of Fame trainer Hirsch Jacobs. The famous Stymie ran in her mother's name and was trained by her father. Before marriage, she had already raced stakes winners Hail to Reason and Regal Gleam.

In 1961, Wolfson decided to get serious, purchased another one thousand acres and began building a showplace farm. In 1964, he acquired Tom Daniels's Broadmoor Farm, mares and foals included. Harbor View was now the largest privately owned farm in Marion County and the second largest in the United States. In seven years, Wolfson runners earned $3,490,571.06, second only to Wheatley Stables in Lexington.

Journalist Neil Maxwell wrote on August 23, 1963, in the *Wall Street Journal* that he enjoyed the sight of Wolfson patrolling his 1,500 acres, representing some $4 million investment, on a bicycle. A seven-furlong track, a house with a pool and tennis courts and expenses that included a $17,000 monthly payroll were impressive for the times.

Louis Wolfson wanted to win the Kentucky Derby in a bad way. Several horses seemed destined to get him there. Since he'd gotten into the business, he'd spent $100,000 for Roving Minstrel from Ocala Stud. The horse won $100,000 the following week and was a major contender for the Derby but then injured himself before the race and had to be destroyed. Another disappointment was Raise a Native, which raced four times and set four track records. He then bowed a tendon and was retired to stud. When Wolfson got the news, he was sitting by his pool at the farm reading the paper. When he was handed the telegram, he read it, wadded it up and tossed it off to the side.

In the spring of 1963, just as Carry Back was winding down his career, Louis Wolfson purchased two Ocala Stud–bred colts at the FBSC sale. The great attractor was the full brother to My Dear Girl, which he obtained for $48,000, the highest price paid in the sale to date. This colt, named Group Leader, broke a shoulder after two races and had to be put down. Wolfson had a right to feel jinxed. But the other horse, which he purchased for $23,500, would more than make up for the disappointment.

This was another tiny Florida-bred that would never get over 15.1 hands. Roman Brother went on to prove that once again, where Florida-breds and size are concerned…don't be concerned. He was soon gelded due to an undescended testicle, so all this diminutive racehorse would ever have to prove would be talent on the track. He would have a long and grueling career, yet he seemed to thrive on hard work. He rapidly proved himself as a 2-year-old with a number of wins in quick succession. Although one of his rivals, Hurry to Market, would earn the championship for 1963, Roman Brother was the nation's leading earnings winner.

By the end of his 3-year-old year, Roman Brother had earned his owner more than $677,000, but his impressive record didn't include the Derby. He had the ill luck to be born in Northern Dancer's and Hill Rise's year. Behind such greats, he finished a very respectable fourth.

He shared the spotlight in 1964 with Sadair, a Dudley and Heath production. This young hotshot would finish his juvenile season with $498,217 in earnings, the most ever earned by a 2-year-old to that date. He had been a measly $10,000 purchase through the FBSC sales. Like Roman Brother, however, he was also nosed out for the championship at the end of the year. However, both these horses helped thrust Ocala Stud (eighth) and D&H Stables (ninth) onto the leading breeders' lists for the year. Ocala Stud was also ranked sixth for number of wins with seventy-one.

At the end of 1965, following three years of campaigning, Roman Brother became the state's first Champion Handicap Horse and its first Horse of the Year. He was also the first horse sold at any public auction to ever make it to Horse of the Year *and* the leading money winner for any horse ever sold through public auction, with a bankroll of $935,203. The 2-year-olds sales could not have had better marketing.

And the farms blossomed again. In 1963, Freeman Keyes started Reverie Knoll, and Isidore Sherman started Farnsworth Farms with five hundred acres. Charles Kieser purchased Forty Oaks Farm from H.A. Jackson, who had carried on a minor breeding operation. Kieser bred Native Street and was an active devotee of the Florida industry until the day he died. Dr. William O. Reed's farm, Mare Haven, was also started. It would become a major stallion station in the following years.

Mrs. Louisa d'A Carpenter built Shoshone Farm, placing her home smack in the middle of her half-mile training track. Apparently she wanted to watch the misty morning workouts from the comforts of her own patio or bed. Leonard Lavin of Alberto-Culver fame purchased the Whitney farm, Greentree Stud, right across from Ocala Stud in the 1960s and renamed it Glen Hill Farm. It still exists. He would eventually produce more than forty stakes winners, with runners earning more than $21 million, and be named Breeder of the Year twice in the 1990s.

The locals loved the influx of wealth and fame. Tourists flocked into the area to see the famous Needles and Carry Back along with the Silver Springs

The Normandy Barn at Live Oak Plantation in 1983. *Photo by Charlene R. Johnson.*

Attraction. Jobs abounded, and land values soared without having to woo heavy industry with smokestacks and fumes. This was a time when someone left their horse tethered out on the front lawn on the outskirts of Ocala with a "For Sale" sign and "Saddle Included" tacked on the saddle blanket, like we might sell cars or motorcycles today.

In the same *Wall Street Journal* article mentioned earlier, Maxwell's heading was, "Race-Horse Breeders in Florida Challenge Kentucky's Dominance." After discussing Wolfson, he went on to describe the plush quarters of the four resident stallions at P.A.B. Widener's Live Oak Plantation, which included an Oriental carpeted hallway between their stalls: "While Mr. Widener's stud barn is unusually lavish, it's only one of scores of impressive stables being erected hereabouts by well-heeled gentlemen. Their activities are producing a new kind of boom for Florida—a rush to get into the business of breeding race horses."

The article pointed out that Mr. Widener came from a long line of Kentucky horsemen and that the Widener Handicap at Hialeah Park was named after his family. "But the new Florida boom is attracting men from a variety of backgrounds. They include industrialist and one-time proxy fighter Louis E. Wolfson, mutual fund president, J.J. Dreyfus, Jr. and Elliott, Robert and Frank Mackle, three brothers noted for their promotion of

Florida retirement communities." The brothers owned Elkcam farm, their name spelled backward.

The article discussed how this boom had transformed thousands of scrub acres in the north-central part of the state into lush green pastures bounded by white board fences. From four farms seven years ago, there were now sixty-two. Uncleared land that sold for $50 per acre seven years ago now sold for $600 or more per acre. Maxwell pointed out that this boom was timely since the demand for more racehorses was growing due to new tracks around the country and longer racing seasons. There had been 33,208 races in 1958, but in 1962, there were 41,711. Purses were growing as well.

Maxwell quoted Vice-President and General Manager of Ocala Stud Joe O'Farrell, who said, "Next year when a lot of the new farms like Mr. Wolfson's and Mr Dreyfus' put their first 2-year-olds on the track, you'll be seeing a lot more Florida winners here and all over the country."

From 1938 to 1958, a total of 645 Florida-breds were registered. Their earnings totaled $7,046,120.00 and averaged $10,924.20. This was an exceptional figure for the times. Yet still, the praise was grudging. Florida-breds were still "outrunning their pedigrees." While pedigrees were improving, bluer blood was the next big challenge for Florida breeders.

Chapter 6

THE KEYLESS LOCK

Many stories exist of the innovative, unusual things that Joe O'Farrell sometimes did. When a mare named Ellen's Best dropped a bay foal by Hail to Reason, Joe O'Farrell's heart sank. Since he foaled virtually every mare himself, he was first to see it. The valuable colt's left rear leg was twisted out of shape, rendering the foal unable to stand and nurse. O'Farrell hated to destroy the unfortunate foal and hated just as much to return the $10,000 stud fee to the mare's owner, Mrs. Ben Cohen, wife of an executive of Pimlico Race Course in Maryland. While waiting for the sun to rise, he drew milk from the mare and fed the struggling foal. Then he phoned the Cohens, asking them to gamble. He had a hunch that he could fix the leg.

He made a splint from an aluminum sweat scraper, bent it to fit the misshapen leg and strapped it on. Every day, he applied a little more tension. Gradually, the leg began to straighten. By the end of the third week, the colt was struggling up on all four wobbly legs and hobbling around his stall.

Joe rang the bell for the second time for a Belmont victory when, in 1965, Hail to All captured that New York race. Billboards all around the county now added Hail to All's name alongside Needles, Carry Back and Roman Brother touting Marion County. He would go on to be a successful stallion.

By 1965, I-75 had connected sleepy little Ocala to the rest of the world of highways, and this would help bring in 1,750,000 visitors to the Silver Springs Attraction alone. A planned improvement was the merger of 301 and 441 just north of Ocala. The controversial Cross State Barge Canal was undergoing construction, with lots of recreation planned along its banks.

Ocala National Forest and the recently opened Six Gun Territory were other lures to central Florida. But the article in the *New York Times* on February 28, 1965, discussing all these attractions was accompanied by a picture of horses running in a field.

Horses were big business. The Commercial Bank and Trust Company of Ocala and its work with horse farms was featured as a cover story in the July issue of the *Burroughs Clearing House* magazine (noted in the July 11, 1965 *Ocala Star-Banner*), a publication for officials of banks and financial institutions. New York banks were sending people to learn from Ocala bank officers how they financed horses and farms.

In February 1965, a reprint from the *Wall Street Journal* in the *Orlando Sentinel* noted that in the fall of 1964, a Keeneland yearling (not a Florida-bred) commanded $170,000, the first time any yearling had topped $100,000. Twenty-seven states permitted parimutuel betting, with the previous year's total betting pool reaching a record $3 billion. To meet the demand, the number of foals produced had a 40 percent increase to about fifteen thousand annually. However, Kentucky's percentage of newborns fell from 29 to 22 percent, most of the loss going to Florida.

On June 27, 1965, Dick Knight stated prophetically in the *Miami Herald* that 150 farms, using some thirty thousand acres scattered around Florida, rivaled Kentucky for the title of "Race Horse Capital of America," while Marion County, the "County the Horse Built," was home to more than half of all those farms. But only in Marion County were the farms large showplaces and valued at some $20 million, while the three thousand Thoroughbreds roaming them were valued at another $30 million. He added that Florida was booming as a standardbred center as well; show horses traveled a regular circuit called the Sunshine Circuit. When other breed figures were factored in, it was clear that the horse, led by the Thoroughbred, had changed land values and the face of central Florida forever.

The successful "Ocala Weekend" was growing too big for the facilities available. In 1966, the Southeastern Pavilion was built. FBSC held the first million-dollar sale in Marion County that year. The "weekend" now extended from Thursday through Sunday, beginning with the meeting of the racing commission, highlighted by the FTBA's awards dinner and ending on Saturday and Sunday with farm tours. The first Annual Turf Writers' Award was won by Jobie Arnold for an article on Ocala Stud Farms published by the *Thoroughbred Record*.

At the awards dinner, which was attended by several state congressmen and county commissioners, Governor Haydon Burns summed up the

FTBA Dinner at the popular Brahma restaurant, October 5, 1962. *From left to right*: Mrs. L.K. Edwards, Carl Rose, Opal Heath, Bonnie Heath and Mrs. Carl Rose. *Photo by Jim Jernigan.*

phenomenal success of the Thoroughbred industry and what it meant for the whole state, later printed in the *Ocala Star Banner*: "The most exciting chapter of the Florida racing industry is being written right here in Marion County by the breeders of thoroughbreds of high quality. The millions of dollars you have invested, the substantial sums you spend in maintaining and operating your breeding farms are a significant contribution to the economic well-being of Florida. The governor of Florida cannot help but be proud of the Florida Thoroughbred Breeders' Association." He mentioned that he had just returned from a visit to the Far East and added, "I can assure you that the names of Needles, Carry Back and Hail to All are as well known in Hong Kong as in Ocala."

Ocala Star Banner columnist John L. Klucina wrote on September 21, 1966, "The Ocala Era is just beginning. In another half century, even sooner, archivists of thoroughbred lore will refer to the mid-60s as 'The Ocala Era.' Just look at the names on the mailboxes along the picturesque rural roads. They include some of America's best known racing and breeding personalities: P.A.B. Widener, III of [Live Oak Plantation], John

Hay Whitney [Greentree Stud], Bruce Campbell [Early Bird Stud], Jack Dreyfuss [Hobeau Farm], Liz Whitney Tippett [Llangollen Farm], William McKnight [Tartan Farms], Louis Wolfson [Harbor View Farm], Mrs. Louisa d'A Carpenter [Shoshone Farm]."

The article went on to say that there were 106 Thoroughbred farms in Marion County with some 5,500 horses living in the county permanently and many more during the training season, September–January. Some $40 million had been invested in property and buildings, with an annual payroll impact of $3.5 million. Another $3 million was spent on the accoutrements of raising horses, feed, bedding and so on. Clearly, the industry was making an impact. Land values had doubled many times over since Needles won the Derby a mere eleven years earlier. The industry was about to take its next leap up the ladder of respectability.

In November 1960, William L. McKnight, chairman of the board of 3M (Minnesota Mining and Manufacturing) and the one who set the management principles of the company from 1949 to 1966, purchased 320 acres of Bonnie Heath's farm, including training track and a barn, and Tartan Farms was born. His philosophy was that if you gave the people a product that would be in every household, you'd do well. He had done just that many times over—Scotch tape, videotape, magnetic sound tape and duct tape later. McKnight was one of the wealthiest men in America.

McKnight had already ventured into the excitement of the racing world, but he hadn't gotten very far by the time his seventieth birthday approached in 1957. His office staff, desperate to find a unique gift for the man who had everything, collected their funds, handed the $6,500 over to McKnight's trainer, John Sceusa, and asked him to find a horse for McKnight. Sceusa purchased Aspidistra, a bad-kneed race mare that had never shown any talent. No one ever knew why he chose her, but it was one of those serendipitous events that changes history.

McKnight apparently felt little sentiment about the strange gift as he sent her out three more times in claiming races (anyone could have purchased her for the value of the race), with no success at either the racing game or of pocketing a handy chunk of change. Doubtless disgusted, he retired her with a total career of two wins in fourteen starts and the meager earnings of $5,115. Little did anyone know what this gift horse would mean, not just to McKnight but to the racing world and, of course, to Florida.

In retrospect, however, it is interesting to note, as Edward L. Bowen pointed out in his book *Matriarchs*, that there was actually a connection to

Florida before Aspidistra ever arrived here. Her dam, Tilly Rose, was one of only two stakes horses ever produced by Bull Brier; the other was Menolene, half-sister to Needles. And in the second race she won, Aspidistra held off by a neck a horse named Rumpled, Rough'n Tumble's full sister.

After a few more years of racing under his tartan plaid silks, another of those serendipitous events, which seemed to so often guide the Florida industry, occurred. Everett Clay, publicity director for Hialeah, informed trainer John Nerud that he thought that McKnight was ready to go big and could use some help. Nerud had earned his trainer's license in 1931 and learned the ropes under world-famous Ben Jones, trainer of six Kentucky Derby winners. When he scoffed that he didn't need any new owners who didn't have money, Clay laughed.

After compiling a dossier on Nerud two and a half inches thick, McKnight accepted the idea. Then began one of the most successful partnerships in the history of racing. Nerud, horse crazy from birth, had a wealth of experience on the tracks already, while McKnight had a wealth of geld. Together, they lacked for nothing. Once McKnight decided to trust Nerud, he handed him the keys and never looked back. Far from a micromanager, he believed in letting a man do the job he was good at.

Nerud immediately convinced McKnight that he needed a farm and that the farm could only be in Lexington, Kentucky, or in Marion County, Florida, the only two places in the world that made sense for raising a decent horse. McKnight, having recently moved to Miami, chose Florida. Nerud was made president of the Tartan Farms Corporation and owned one-fourth of the business, which included all the racing stock. One of his first moves was to hire an Irish trainer raised on the Curragh named John H. Hartigan to be the farm manager. This freed him up to continue training and seeking good horses on the track. The triumvirate took off.

They quickly purchased another seven hundred acres, and immediate construction and reconstruction turned the farm into the most state-of-the-art modern facilities anywhere in the world. Split-log fencing gave the farm a unique appearance. McKnight's (or 3M's) contribution of the first all-weather, synthetic track, Astro Turf, was also tested at Tropical Park and for a short time became the standard as the safest surface for racetracks at that time. Since it was also slow, however, it didn't last long.

Hartigan, six-foot-six, with a swagger like a Texan (complete with Stetson), oversaw the farm efficiently. It was his job to maintain the farm and raise the babies until they were old enough to come under Nerud's guidance at the tracks. Like many breeders before him, Hartigan credited the land. In

Tartan barn sign that was taken off one of the barns when Tartan was sold. It's now hanging in the FTBOA offices. *Photo by Charlene R. Johnson.*

Tartan Farms. *Courtesy* The Florida Horse.

Tartan Track Aerial. *Courtesy* The Florida Horse.

an interview for the January 15, 1968 *Morning Telegraph*, he said, "I've raised horses in England, Ireland, Arizona, Kentucky, Virginia and Colorado, and I'm convinced there is something in Florida that they don't have anywhere else. We don't have the first idea of what it is, but it must be in the grass. It can't be in the sun because they raise great horses in Ireland and England and where could you find a more cloudy and damp climate? And we're no better feeders here than in Kentucky, Virginia or California. Horsemen are horsemen the world over. But the horses we raise here outrun their pedigrees. No two ways about it."

The first horses to arrive at the farm were a few mares, including Aspidistra. Although bred to a ho-hum stallion, she had already produced a minor winner that went on later to produce two stakes winners. Next Nerud bred her to a stallion named First Cabin. That mating produced a stakes winner named A. Deck, which earned a healthy career bankroll of $126,185. Aspidistra met Needles the following year, getting Chinatowner, winner of the Canadian Turf Handicap at Gulfstream Park. The dubious gift mare was beginning to shine.

Intentionally. *Painting by Angie Draper.*

Once the farm was launched, Nerud's next job was to find a top-grade stallion prospect. He found Harry Isaacs's Intentionally, already winner of many stakes and holder of track records, as well as voted Champion Sprinter of 1959. Under Nerud, he would also be pushed to win over a distance. Although McKnight hesitated one full moment, he showed faith in Nerud yet again by coughing up a heart-stopping $750,000 for the purchase in 1961. Nerud "intentionally" ran the horse three more times just so McKnight could get pictures in the winner's circle with the horse. Then, in 1962, Intentionally, co-holder with Swaps of a world record for a mile, was retired to Tartan Farms with career earnings of $752,258. He was syndicated for $750,000 at thirty shares for $25,000 each.

He was perfect for Florida, but he was also perfect for Nerud, who always bred for speed first yet also chose for the ability to go some distance. Nerud then begged Frances Genter to send My Dear Girl to his new acquisition, and thus started another longtime partnership between the Genters and Tartan Farms.

On April 4, 1964, Tilley noted in the *Daily Racing Form* that "Florida-bred, My Dear Girl, champion 2-year-old filly of her year has foaled a

My Dear Girl with In Reality in 1964. *Courtesy* The Florida Horse.

handsome colt by Intentionally at Tartan Farms. The mare, owned by Mrs. Frances Genter, is being bred to Ambehaving." On May 23, he wrote, "John Hartigan tells us that 14 of the Intentionally foals on the ground thus far are out of stakes winners, stake producers or stakes-placed winners." Lesser pedigrees would never again be an issue in Florida.

Tartan Farms was about to be launched into the spotlight with that extraordinary 1964 crop. Two Rough'n Tumble colts, Minnesota Mac and Ruffled Feathers, would become great racehorses. The result of the Intentionally–My Dear Girl cross was a small, handsomely made bay colt that would be named In Reality. Like *The Wizard of Oz* in the year of *Gone with the Wind*, In Reality, as brilliant as he was, would not be considered best. But since the best also came from this farm, he helped ensure the success of Tartan Farms.

The gift horse Aspidistra had been bred to Rough'n Tumble. When this bay colt arrived on April 6, 1964, he was a tangle of long, long legs and gangly corners. A youth named Al Roberts was there at his birth and would be there at his death, a constant companion. But neither he nor Nerud knew just what they had yet. They feared that his awkward, long-bodied proportions meant that he might always be too skinny and ungainly. The

Aspidistra and Dr. Fager. *Painting by Angie Draper.*

fact that he took longer than most foals just to stand and nurse seemed a bad omen. He also had two clubfeet, which meant he would not go to the sales. So from the start, he was destined to try his luck under the McKnight tartan.

This colt gained his name from Nerud, who, due to a racetrack injury, nearly died from a blood clot on the brain. In gratitude to the surgeon who saved his life, he named the horse after him, Dr. Fager. This would be one of very few non-Sioux names for Nerud horses. Nerud, who owned thirteen thousand acres of the Black Hills in South Dakota, was fond of Sioux names, so most of his horses sported such names as Black Pipe, Ta Wee (Beautiful Girl) and Ee Noc O Nee (Hurry Up).

Along with the other future stars, the blood-bay colt learned the ropes of maneuvering under tack and around a track as a fall yearling. Gangly and awkward though he might be, the colt was an eager learner. He wanted to please and always gave his best. Besides his great talent, the other thing everyone most remembers about him was his sensitivity. He hated to be yelled at or whipped, which certainly didn't happen often. It truly seemed to hurt his feelings. He was gentle with everyone, including a litter of kittens born in his stall. He was extraordinarily careful not to step on them and

John Nerud and Dr. Fager. *Courtesy* The Florida Horse.

would drop his nose to check on them when first entering. This gentleness continued even when he became a stallion.

Gradually he learned to coordinate those mile-long legs. As he gained both coordination and confidence, and as he continued to fill out his angular frame, his handlers began to like what they saw: a ground-eating stride, great heart and a willingness to run when asked…but then, get out of the way. Once asked, the horse was nearly impossible to stop, something that sometimes got future jockeys in trouble and taken off the horse.

The four Tartan horses trained alongside one another; but although it was comical to see diminutive In Reality next to the towering giant Dr. Fager, it was clear that the tough little colt did not lack a thing but size. Although he never did get his nose in front of Dr. Fager, he helped drive the bigger horse to many of his wins. Although it made for great Florida-bred and Tartan Farms news to have two such greats running, often in the same races, Dr. Fager's true competition throughout his career was Kentucky-bred Damascus, one of the finest ever to race out of the Bluegrass State. He, even more than In Reality, would feel the keen disappointment of usually the groomsman, not the groom.

Dr. Fager's first start is worth a description from his jockey's viewpoint by author Steve Haskin in his book *Dr. Fager.* This was a five-and-a-half-furlong maiden race at Aqueduct on July 15, a late start by Florida standards. Nerud didn't think the horse really fit yet and just wanted to try him. Thus he gave the horse's regular exercise rider the ride. David Hidalgo was only an apprentice rider but knew the horse better than any other rider at that point. Nerud wasn't especially loyal to jockeys, so the big colt would ultimately break in a lot of jocks as to what a real racehorse was all about.

Dr. Fager broke onto what was considered a dead racetrack, and Hidalgo grabbed for him, startled. Although near the end of the pack, it was a tightly bunched group, so no one was very far behind. Dr. Fager simply started bulling through the pack. Hidalgo, in Haskin's words,

> *was standing up on him like a water skier just to keep him from running over top of horses. Nearing the quarter pole, Hidalgo ranged up alongside Walter Blum.*
>
> *I'm yelling "Whoa," on my horse and I look over and Blum is driving his horse! As I'm yelling "Whoa!!" I'm blowing by Blum. I couldn't believe it!...It was all I could do to get him to only win by seven!*

Dr. Fager would exhibit incredible talent for the next three years, but Nerud's talent was also highlighted. While In Reality and Dr. Fager continued their war, which at one point had Dr. Fager reaching over to savage the cheeky little horse trying to sneak up on his inside, it was Damascus and, occasionally, Buckpasser against which he fought his best duels. Although he literally flew to several stakes victories in his 2-year-old year, the World Playground and Cowdin Stakes, he could also get caught up in speed duels that would burn him out before the end. Once rolling in pursuit of, or to keep ahead of, a foe, jocks found it difficult to convince him to do otherwise. Competing trainers quickly learned this and, throughout his career, sent "rabbits" out to lure him to an early burnout, a tactic that worked a few times.

In their 3-year-old year, In Reality earned a chance at the Derby when he won both the Fountain of Youth and the Florida Derby. However, at that point, Sunshine Calvert made the controversial decision not to start the small colt in the Kentucky Derby, stating that it was just too much, too early to ask a young horse to do.

In December 26, 1967, Joe Hirsch's column in the *Morning Telegraph* quoted a prophetic Sunshine Calvert, "I believe In Reality will make a superior stallion when he is retired. He's got intelligence and spirit, breeding and speed, and that's a lot of plusses to start with."

Dr. Fager, Manuel Ycaza up. *Courtesy* The Florida Horse.

Coming up on the Derby, the ratio of Florida-bred potentials to all other horses with a decent chance was astonishingly high. Besides In Reality and Dr. Fager, other Florida-breds proving themselves included Diplomat Way, winner of the Arlington-Washington Futurity and second in the Louisiana Derby; Tumble Wind, second in the Santa Anita Derby, undefeated as a 2-year-old; Brunch, who also came from Tartan Farms; and several more. Yet oddly enough, neither of the two brightest stars started.

Sunshine Calvert gave his colt a rest and then put blinkers on In Reality for his 1968 season. Mrs. Genter's colt shaved a full second off the track record in the Campbell Prep at Bowie in Maryland for a mile and sixteenth on April 13, 1968. He then captured the Campbell Handicap at the same distance and track, beating Barb's Delight and carrying a heavy 122 pounds. He met up with Dr. Fager's usual nemesis in the $200,000, ninety-second running of the Preakness, where he ran a game second to Damascus, the horse that would earn the 2-year-old Championship of 1967.

Meanwhile, Dr. Fager's equally headstrong trainer made the controversial decision to skip the Triple Crown races altogether. After beating the rising star Damascus in the one-mile Gotham, a disappointed public had been looking forward to a virtual match race in the Derby. They would get their hearts' desire, but not in the Triple Crown races.

Damascus missed in the Derby but captured the next two legs of the coveted crown. While a horse named Proud Clarion won that Derby, Dr. Fager scooted home first in the Withers. Perhaps Nerud's brightest hour that year was when he managed two horses winning $100,000 races on the same day: Dr. Fager in the Hawthorne Gold Cup and Ruffled Feathers in the Man o' War at Aqueduct.

On August 29, 1967, Chuck Tilley reported new figures for the preceding year in the *Morning Telegraph*. Six of the nation's fifteen leading Thoroughbred breeders were Florida-based operations: Llangollen Farm, Hobeau Farm, Tartan Farms, Harbor View, Mrs. Frances Genter's racing stable and Ocala Stud. Four of the leading stallions on the General Sire lists were Florida stallions: Intentionally, Beau Gar, Rough'n Tumble and Needles. Petare was also high on the 2-year-old list, while Rough'n Tumble, which had only half as many performers as any stallion ranked above him, was moving high onto the broodmare sire list. By the end of the year, Tartan Farms had become Florida's leading breeder with total earnings of $1,048,808, and it was ranked fourth nationally, with Hobeau and Harbor View hot on its heels. For the first time ever, a Florida owner led the nation's owner lists. Jack Dreyfuss's Hobeau Farms was the nation's leading owner by money won, with earnings of $1,120,443.

Four of the nation's top 3-year-olds were Florida-breds: Tartan Farms' Dr. Fager, Mrs. Frances Genter's In Reality, Llangollen Farm's Tumble Wind and Harvey Peltier's Diplomat Way. Jack Dreyfus Jr.'s Handsome Boy was at the top of the handicap division thanks to beating the 1966 Horse of the Year, Buckpasser. Mrs. Vanderbilt Adams's Desert Trial and Harbor View Farm's Swinging Mood were giving the older mares a run for their money. Finally, Dr. Fager finished his 1967 3-year-old season as Florida's first national Champion Sprinter.

In October 1967, the FBSC established its first national record when a weanling sold for $47,000. On November 17, 1967, Tilley wrote in the *Miami Herald*, "In their wildest imaginations, the first of the Florida breeders couldn't have dreamed it would have happened so quickly...but to have raised almost 30 percent of the winners of the $100,000-added races in America with less than five percent of the horses now in training!"

Although barely nosed out of the 2-year-old and 3-year-old Colt Championships, it was in his fourth year that no one could stop Dr. Fager—not jockeys, not competing horses and not racing secretaries piling on more weight than anyone could believe possible for a horse to carry in the kind of grueling competition he was given.

* THE ARLINGTON CLASSIC *
TARTAN STABLE   Mile (VALUE $106,000) 1-36   J.A. NERUD-trainer
owner   BRAULIO BAEZA   up
LIGHTNING ORPHAN 2nd D R. F A G E R   JUNE 24, 1967
DIPLOMAT WAY   3rd ARLINGTON   PARK   Kuprion photo

Dr. Fager in winner's circle. McKnight is in the center, and Nerud to his left, with Mr. and Mrs. Binger. *Courtesy* The Florida Horse.

"The Keyless Lock" was the headline created by Charles Hatton of the *Morning Telegraph* just before the Roseben in early May 1968 after watching the Doc's sizzling workouts. The idea of trying to find the key to pick the lock that Dr. Fager had on the race was repeated by many turf writers. The key was still missing as he scored by three lengths carrying 130 pounds.

Over the Fourth of July holiday in 1968, the Suburban Handicap at Aqueduct was touted as the race of the year, with the three greats against one another: Dr. Fager, Damascus and In Reality. It would be the third time that Dr. Fager and Damascus would come together, each having beaten the other once. Dr. Fager won, while In Reality brought up the rear, burned out by the rabbit, Hedevar.

Dr. Fager sped to a world record in the Washington Park Handicap on August 24, 1968, winning by 10.5 lengths and carrying 134 pounds, the most ever carried in the race. Just before this race, he was syndicated to stand at stud for the 1969 season, with a projected value of $3,200,000. Five outside shares had already been sold for $100,000 each. Sixteen shares would be retained by McKnight and Nerud. The purchases were notably Bluegrass: Whitney, Phipps, Guest, Dupont, Vanderbilt and more. After this race, Nerud was heard to say, "No single horse can beat Dr. Fager right now."

In his entire career, only three horses ever finished in front of Dr. Fager: Champion 2-Year-Old Colt Successor, once; Horse of the Year Damascus, twice; and Horse of the Year Buckpasser, once, in the same race Damascus won. In twenty-two races, Dr. Fager failed to earn the trophy only three times and only finished as "badly" as third once. He earned one disqualification, which set him out of the money, but he had finished first. By the end of 1968, Dr. Fager was voted four championships in a single year, a feat never yet duplicated: Champion Sprinter, Champion Grass Horse, Champion Handicap Horse and Horse of the Year, Florida's second. He became Florida's second millionaire with earnings of $1,002,642; he set three records and equaled a fourth. It would be some thirty years before a few of those records would ever be broken. He could go a distance, he could charge in sprints and he could run on dirt or turf. He could do it all and do it easily. Although others have earned as many championships over more than one year, even the great Secretariat would earn only three in 1973.

Dr. Fager is considered one of the most versatile and talented horses of all times. And running second to him three times was tough, little In Reality. Florida took home two more championships in 1968: Process Shot won Champion 2-Year-Old Filly, and Top Knight won Champion 2-Year-Old Colt. Tartan Farms and the Florida breeding industry had their place in the sun and in the nation.

When his racing career was over and he was shipping back to stand at stud at Tartan, Dr. Fager's van was met at the county line by Marion County

Dr. Fager, painted on brown wrapping paper. *Painting by Angie Draper.*

Dr. Fager is no. 1. *Courtesy* The Florida Horse.

deputy sheriff Don Moreland, who solemnly approached Dr. Fager's head and presented him with a ticket for "reckless speed."

When the announcement came out regarding the national championships, December 8, 1968, was declared Dr. Fager Day in Ocala, observed at Tartan Farms. Agricultural Commissioner Doyle Conner was the guest speaker, while the star galloped around the track for the visitors. About 1,200 central Floridians showed up to see Dr. Fager receive a plaque from the Department of Agriculture and made a member of the Marion County Chamber of Commerce.

Doing well had its repercussions, however. Tartan had been formed as a subchapter S corporation, meaning it could maintain the advantages of a corporation while being taxed as a partnership, each partner responsible for his own gains and losses. In 1967, both McKnight and Nerud owed $250,000 in taxes. McKnight took the matter to court, and it was settled that Nerud did not have to pay his share, but he did have to give up his one-quarter share in Tartan. He retained his interest in Dr. Fager and continued as president to the end of Tartan Farms.

This really was a dream partnership. Nerud turned in a weekly report, and that was that. He had virtually a free rein. Some fifteen years or so into the partnership, with McKnight advancing in age, Nerud, never shy, suggested to McKnight that he might want to will his horses to his daughter, Virginia, and son-in-law, James Binger…so that Nerud would be ensured an ongoing job. Shortly after that, Nerud received a letter from McKnight informing him that all of his horses had been transferred to his daughter's name and that Nerud would be taking orders from her from now on.

Both In Reality and Dr. Fager retired to Tartan Farms in 1969. Both would prove to be strong foundational sires of champions and great broodmares. In Reality would ultimately win this race, however, since Dr. Fager died too young of a twisted intestine in 1976. Still, he was posthumously named Sire of the Year for earnings in 1977; he sired thirty-five stakes winners.

Both became the most important horses to influence Florida breeding for decades to come. In Reality was not My Dear Girl's only good racehorse, but he carried on both racing talent and bloodlines, making himself Florida's next strong foundation sire. The repercussions of this one remarkable bloodline would run strong into modern day. He sired champions and Hall of Famers Desert Vixen, Smile, Known Fact and Relaunch, among many others. But he was also known as a great broodmare sire. His dams produced champion, Meadow Star and Kentucky's Broodmare of the Year in 1993, Toussaud. By 1984, In Reality's stud fee had reached $80,000, and he was still standing at Tartan. At a time when stallions that became successful were often shipped off to Kentucky or more lucrative breeding areas, where they could command higher prices and attract better-blooded mares, this was a feat in itself.

In 1971, Dr. Fager became the first Florida-bred to be inducted into the National Racing Museum's Hall of Fame in Saratoga Springs, New York. In 1972, his trainer would be inducted right behind him. He had trained twenty-seven stakes winners and five champions, including Dr. Fager and the full sister of Dr. Fager, Ta Wee, which became Sprint Champion in 1969 and 1970 while carrying weights reminiscent of her brother's. Ta Wee would produce Great Above, a great stakes horse and sire of 1994 Horse of the Year Holy Bull.

Aspidistra had clearly earned her place in the famous Tartan equine graveyard. Like Ocala Stud, a large cemetery still exists on the old Tartan property. There lie many of the Tartan champions: Aspidistra, Dr. Fager, Ta Wee, Intentionally, My Dear Girl, Codex, Dark Mirage, Minnesota Mac, Gentle Touch, Your Alibhai, Dr. Patches and Cequillo.

By 1986, Tartan Farms had been at the top of the breeders' lists for eighteen years. In 1987, Tartan Farms stock was dispersed, and a legacy that

THE FALL HIGHWEIGHT HANDICAP
BELMONT PARK $ 25,000 ADDED AUG. 25. 1969
TARTAN STABLE " TA WEE " J.L. ROTZ up
F.S. SCHULHOFER trainer   6 Fur. Time 1'10:1
KING EMPEROR 2 nd Pres. By Mr. Frank M. Basil GAYLORDS FEATHER 3 rd

Ta Wee winning the Fall Highweight Handicap. *Photo by Mike Sirico.*

doubtless will never be matched passed into the annals of history. Part of the farm was sold to Harry Mangurian, who created Mockingbird Farm. Then in 2001, Mockingbird was sold and turned into Winding Oaks Farm.

Tartan and its principles were responsible for breeding more than one hundred stakes winners and several champions. While Rosemere Farm and then Ocala Stud Farms launched the Florida Thoroughbred industry into being, it could rightly be said that it was Tartan Farms that carried it to the stars.

Nerud, who continued to be an influential trainer, later admitted that he had originally hoped that McKnight would choose Kentucky since that was where the nation's stallions were. He added in an interview in the late '80s, "Kentucky will always have the stallions, but Florida breeds a tougher, better horse than Kentucky. I've never figured that one out. They're tough and they can run, but I don't know why!"

Both McKnight and his gift horse died in 1978; she was twenty-four and he ninety. Nerud, in 2013, was living in New York and at the age of one hundred still going to the track in the mornings.

WHEN NODOUBLE WON the Arkansas Derby on the same day In Reality captured the Campbell Handicap (April 20, 1968), it made for more cheering.

His sire, Australian champion *Noholme II, stood at Bob Marks's Robin's Nest Farm and was the leading national sire of 2-year-olds the previous year. His acceptance was immediate as proven by the great book of mares sent his way from the start. When Nodouble retired to Florida, he, too, would become a leading sire for the state, but even better, he was a Florida model.

The rest of the world was discovering the beauty to be found in central Florida. In April 1968, Ocala photographer Jim Jernigan was chosen by William A. Reedy of Eastman Kodak Company to shoot a number of the county's Thoroughbred farms as backgrounds for international advertising. Jernigan was one of only 250 photographers nationwide to have been asked to participate with Kodak in its publications for the previous ten years. Three days of filming at Ocala Stud, Live Oak Stud, Tartan Farms, Dorchester Equine Preparatory School, Pinecrest Farm and Echo Dell Farm resulted in more than one thousand photographs, from which fifteen to twenty would be chosen for two new publications called *Applied Photography* and *Commercial Camera*.

In an article in the *Ocala Star Banner* on April 21, 1968, Reedy stated, "We came through Ocala last year and saw the horse farms for the first time. Their beauty of setting, with the oak trees and Spanish moss, the free rolling openness of the land caught our camera eye." He then visited Lexington and added, "In our opinion, the Lexington area didn't have the exotic appeal to the camera

The ballet of the horses at Tartan Farm in 1967. *Photo by Jim Jernigan.*

that Ocala has. Here the horses seem to put on a continuous ballet as they move constantly about the paddocks. The newness and clean-cut appearance of the farms offers something that has never been available to the commercial advertising illustrator." He expected their work of the three days to be the subject of "many advertising illustrations in years to come."

Later in June, *Vogue* magazine descended to the horse farms as well. Its photographers were shooting for an article depicting Florida as something more than just sand and sea. And in October, Charles Kuralt of the Walter Cronkite show brought a TV crew down to shoot footage on Ocala Stud, Tartan Farms and Diamond C Farms, among others. They also planned to attend the sales.

THE ELEVENTH ANNUAL 2-year-old sale, held on January 31, 1968, was a huge success, with a record-breaking sales topper of $154,000 and an average of $14,608, well up over the previous year's average of $10,062. It was also a record year for first-time buyers and for attendance in general. "The development of this new market area benefits the entire national industry," wrote Tilley in the *Morning Telegraph* of March 6, 1968.

On January 27, 1968, Joe Hirsch, another popular *Morning Telegraph* columnist, wrote enthusiastically, "The Florida breeders put on quite a show here this week. They have not only the best and most attractive sales ring in America, but they have one of the very best markets, and they are selling some fine race horses…Florida breeders have made some tremendous strides in a handful of years. Theirs is a story without parallel in American racing and breeding annals. Propelled by the enthusiasm and energetic activity of Joe O'Farrell, they did it by upgrading their bloodstock and developing their own stars. They merit the industry's admiration."

Following this sale, Fasig-Tipton and Florida breeders held a sale for mostly out-of-state horses. By March, they had conducted three venues of 2-year-olds in training. All told, they took in $5 million in the five-week period. "You could never have imagined it five years ago," John Finney said to Tilley in the *Morning Telegraph* on March 6, 1968. In addition, the FBSC-sponsored breeding stock sale in Ocala in October generated $1 million, and everyone agreed that it was getting better every year.

On September 15, 1968, it was announced that Peter A.B. Widener was selling the 1,064-acre Live Oak Stud to Charlotte Colket of Philadelphia, heiress to the Campbell Soup fortune. Widener transferred his stock to his Kentucky farm. Charlotte (Colket) Weber has been the mistress of this beautiful farm ever since. Her distinctive red, black and white silks have raced to victory in many top graded stakes. Her son, Chester, is host to one of the premier combined driving events in the United States. They also run cattle and other equine breeds on the farm.

In 1966, the FTBA finally moved into its own building at the Golden Hills Golf and Turf Club. By 1968, it had unveiled, during Ocala Week, the Florida Horse Hall of Fame. O'Farrell had discovered an equine artist trained at the Ringling School of Art and Design, Angie Draper, and labelled her "an artist who knows horses." Angie's first portraits began with thirteen charter members: Rough'n Tumble, Noodle Soup (dam of Needles), Iltis (dam of My Dear Girl), Joppy (dam of Carry Back), Roman Zephyr (dam of Roman Brother), Aspidistra (dam of Dr. Fager), Needles, Carry Back, My Dear Girl, Hail to All, Dr. Fager, Roman Brother and In Reality. Angie would continue to paint champions and important horses for the FTBA as they were produced, to be added to the growing collection on the walls into the 1990s. The breeding industry in Florida finally had a permanent home.

Chapter 7

HORSE FEVER

In 1970, the ladies led the way, earning three championships for the Sunshine State breeders: Dr. Fager's little sister, Ta Wee, was named Champion Sprinter for the second year in a row, while Forward Gal, bred by Abraham "Butch" Savin and raced by his Aisco Stable, was named Champion 2-Year-Old Filly. Office Queen, bred by Steven Calder, who was about to open the new Calder Race Course in south Florida, which would begin summer racing in Florida, was named Champion 3-Year-Old Filly.

Louis Wolfson's Harbor View Farm became the nation's Leading Breeder by Money Won, with total earnings of $1,515,861, making Florida only the third state to top this list. It duplicated the feat in 1971 with earnings of $1,739,214. It also won the award for Leading Breeder by Races Won in 1970 at 366, in 1971 with 394 and again in 1972 with 326 wins. Hobeau Farm was hot on its heels as the second leading breeder nationally by money won, losing to its state-mate by a mere $23,118 in 1971. It had been bad enough in 1967 when Hobeau Farm led the nation's owner's lists. One could claim that blue-blooded horses helped it accomplish that feat, but a breeder generally breeds on his or her own farm.

By 1972, other states were using the FTBA model to form or revamp their own breeder organizations. The FTBA maintained a field office at one of the tracks to assist in the collection of the funds to go into the breeders' awards. At least one race per day was being run just for Florida-breds. It maintained a well-stocked library for its members, including a new microfiche library. It welcomed tour groups and coordinated the gala Ocala Week program in October, the January Awards Dinner in Miami, the Tampa Weekend program held in conjunction with the running of the Breeders' Futurity at Florida Downs and many other functions. It had representation on the governor's Florida Thoroughbred Advisory Board. Its mantra at this time was "Where the Horse World's Going."

The industry had changed much over the years. From passionate believers in the earliest years, it had evolved into a serious investment and financial business for many who were in it by the 1970s. The one thing that remained the same was that it was a moneyed industry. There is a reason why they call horseracing the "Sport of Kings"—it takes money. Not everyone did it for the love of the animal. Some of the wealthiest people in the world used their equine businesses for tax write-offs, hobbies or investments.

Marion County, the heart of the Thoroughbred industry by the 1970s, was host to many big farms owned by wealthy folks. Most of them did not live on their farms. A divide had begun to occur between the horse people and the community. They lived in two different worlds. Because many of the farm owners only stopped by on their way to somewhere else or to check on their investments, the community did not get to know them. The county and city of Ocala could not fail to cheer when a home-bred won, but it was the pride of place more than a pride of the animal, farm or owner. More than one native-born in Marion County admitted that while they remember being bussed out to Bonnie Heath Farm to see Needles, they'd never touched a horse, far less ridden one, and they had no idea what the industry as a whole was all about. Most of the county's population worked hard just to survive. The luxury of a racehorse was beyond conception. As the horses grew in value and spread in

Stavola Farm in 1970. *Photo by Jim Jernigan.*

Lin-Drake in 1970. *Photo by Jim Jernigan.*

fame, and as people came from all over the world to purchase better and better bloodlines and proven talent, the rift widened.

Tilley wrote in *The Florida Horse* in 1976, "The majority of farm owners still are absentees, men still engaged in business elsewhere and not yet ready to retire to full time horse farming." He quoted one owner saying that he "loved the farm but they can't just drop everything to raise race horses."

Some horsemen and horsewomen who arrived about this time would remain active parts of the industry and community for years. In 1972, billionaire George Steinbrenner, owner of the New York Yankees and a global shipping business, bought Tampa Bay Downs and purchased Robin's Nest Farm west of Ocala, where he began raising racehorses on his renamed Kinsman Stud; as of 2014, it is run by his daughter. With all he had done in his life, he once said, "There is no thrill in the world like winning a horse race."

Harry Mangurian put it another way: "Of all my business endeavors, breeding and racing thoroughbred horses has been the most challenging." As the owner of Southeastern Jet and Drexel Investments, among many other businesses, he grew Mockingbird Farms to 1,100 acres and a major breeding and racing presence in the national industry. Like Tartan before him, he would stand many of Florida's best stallions over the years, including Valid Appeal, Diablo, Storm Creek and Rizzi. He bred and/or raced some

Desert Vixen winning the Makette. *Courtesy* The Florida Horse.

150 stakes winners, including two-time Eclipse Award winner Desert Vixen. By 2000, Harry Mangurian had won more Eclipse Awards as top owner and breeder in the nation than even Fred Hooper.

In 1973, the same year Secretariat won the 3-year-old Male and Grass Horse Championships, Florida matched his three with three of its own: Desert Vixen won the 3-Year-Old Filly award and Susan's Girl the Handicap Mare Championship. Shecky Greene, a *Noholme II colt, was named Champion Sprinter.

Dan Lasater, who made a fortune in the fast-food business and retired at twenty-three, bought Maverick Farm, which had evolved from Sunshine Stud, and turned it into Lasater Farm in 1973. In fast fashion once again, he quickly built up a large band of broodmares and a respectable stallion roster. In just a few years after his first race, he jumped to the top ranks of the nation's leading owners and breeders while admitting that he was not sentimental about horses—he ran farm and racing stables as a business. That long-awaited, giant stride Hobeau had taken to reach that Leading Owner list, Lasater took so fast and so often that it could hardly be credited. He led the owners' lists from 1973 to 1976 by money won and from 1974 to

The twelfth annual Baby Show. *Photo by Joe Migon, courtesy Coady Photography/Hialeah archives.*

1977 by races won. In 1974, he became the first owner ever to surpass the $2 million mark in earnings. His crash was just as spectacular, however, when in 1984 he ran into legal problems and sold his farm to a group of people (including John Fernung) that renamed it Southland Farm.

Richard Irwin, a textbook publisher, purchased the old Elkcam farm and turned it into Lin-Drake Farm. Karl Koontz became its general manager. That farm would later become Adena Springs. Wycombe House Stud, Good Chance Farm, Marablue Training Center, Meadowbrook Farms, Gateway Farm, Fayview Farm, Mare Haven Farm and Lavery Farm…the names are lovely and reminiscent of a wonderful, almost romantic era. The people, incoming farms and new equine stars are far too numerous to name them all. Most would last into the 1980s, only a few beyond. While the industry nationwide saw a foal crop growth of 70 percent, in Florida the increase was 220 percent. The Jockey Club in April 1974 told Chuck Tilley in his *DRF* column, "The rate of increase is the greatest that has ever been recorded by any state in history."

In 1974, membership in the FTBA reached a record high of 645, and Ocala Week was now a true, full week. It included a charity golf tournament, turf writers' breakfast, awards dinner, the Fillies Follies and more big news:

Abraham I. "Butch" Savin, owner of Aisco Stud, announced that he would stand Mr. Prospector in Florida. This talented horse had been runner-up to greats like Secretariat and Forego and was considered a top-class pedigree with great conformation. Since Kentucky wanted him, Florida breeders applauded Savin's decision to bring him to Florida. Shares were valued at $50,000, with a fee of $7,500. He would quickly prove himself indeed to be a top sire.

Among the many outstanding breeders and leaders of the 1970s was Waldemar Farms, created by Howard W. Sams and his son, Tim. This farm is representative of a spreading industry. As Marion County real estate escalated in value, development prices began making it tougher to stay agricultural. New farms began spreading and sprouting into surrounding counties. Waldemar was located near Williston in neighboring Levy County. Sams brought What a Pleasure to Florida, one more stallion that further boosted the pedigrees of Florida-breds and proved to be another great bloodline that carried forward for years.

With the coming of stallions like Intentionally, What a Pleasure, Mr. Prospector and many more, no one heard anymore that Florida-breds outran their pedigrees, nor was it rare for the youngsters to show up in the best yearling sales rings. Foolish Pleasure, a colt by What a Pleasure, was bred by Waldemar Farms and sent to the Saratoga Yearling Sales. The bay colt was purchased by John L. Greer for $20,000 and then broken and trained at eighty-year-old Bruce Campbell's Early Bird Stud Farm.

Foolish Pleasure soon became a hit when he won all seven of his races as a 2-year-old. He was named Champion 2-Year-Old Colt in 1974, the same year a Kentucky-bred filly named Ruffian was named Champion 2-Year-Old

Foolish Pleasure winning the Kentucky Derby in 1975. *Courtesy* The Florida Horse.

Filly. His only failure before the Kentucky Derby of 1975 was in the Florida Derby, when he incurred a foot injury and finished third to Prince Thou Art and Sylvan Place. By the time he won the Kentucky Derby, firmly trouncing the only two horses ever to beat him, it was his eleventh win in twelve starts, and he had a bankroll of $673,515. However, he lost both the Preakness and the Belmont, dashing hopes for Florida's first Triple Crown.

Nonetheless, he was considered best of his time, as was Ruffian, the "Queen of the Fillies" who was undefeated in ten races. In July 1975, a match race was arranged between the two horses. Since they both had ridden the same jockey, Jacinto Vasquez was forced to choose; he chose Ruffian. Braulio Baeza happily grabbed the ride on Foolish Pleasure.

Ruffian was much beloved by the public, as talented fillies often are. Called the "Battle of the Sexes," this race was compared to another such battle taking place at the same time on the tennis court between Billie Jean King and Bobby Riggs. It was one of the most heart-rending races ever, and it was viewed by a huge crowd, at the track and on television. The great filly broke her leg but refused to stop running, badly damaging it. When, following surgery, she panicked and further damaged it, she was euthanized. The wailing was heard around the world. It would be some time before trainers would risk a good filly in an open or male-dominated race again.

Foolish Pleasure was inducted into the National Museum of Racing and Hall of Fame in 1995. His trainer, Leroy Jolley, said, "Secretariat is the greatest horse I ever saw; Foolish Pleasure is the greatest horse I ever had."

What a Pleasure was America's leading sire in 1975, while Waldemar led breeders by average earnings. What a Pleasure's title was a result not just of Foolish Pleasure but also of his next rising star, Honest Pleasure.

Another bay colt sent to the Saratoga Yearling Sales, this one sold for $45,000 to Bert and Diana Firestone. He followed in his half-brother's footsteps when he, too, was named Champion 2-Year-Old Colt of 1975, joining other state-breds Dearly Precious as Champion 2-Year-Old Filly and Susan's Girl, which once again at age six captured Champion Handicap Mare honors. She also became the first female ever to break the million-dollar mark.

Just before the 1975 Kentucky Derby, the following was written by Gerald Strine (the author's writing mentor while both worked at the *Horsemen's Journal*) for *Sports Illustrated* on February 16, 1976:

These are times that try Kentuckians' souls. It was insult enough that Foolish Pleasure, a horse born and bred 700 miles from God's bluegrass, won the 1975 Kentucky Derby. It is gross insolence that another colt sired by the same stallion standing in the same upstart locality—Williston, Florida, sir—should be the winter book favorite for the Kentucky Derby for 1976. And it is offensive to anyone with julep in his veins that this Florida stallion is the nation's leading sire; not only that, but a son of the venerated Bold Ruler who could become what his daddy was—the top sire for nearly a decade. Who, in short, could turn out to be the best of the Bold Rulers at stud.

To make the matter even more repugnant to Kentuckians, this potent stallion reached the top of the money list with the help of some of the commonest little numbers in horsedom. Until the dam of Foolish Pleasure came along—a decent sort—our sire had no quality mares to help him.

The name of this impertinent animal is What a Pleasure, and he stands at something called Waldemar Farm, whose master is one Tim Sams. Oh, yes, What a Pleasure has another 3-year-old, Whatsyourpleasure, rated only three pounds below the top-weighted Honest Pleasure in the Experimental Free Handicap. Which is to say, two of the top five candidates for classic honors this year are What a Pleasure's sons. No other stallion on earth is so richly represented.

Although Honest Pleasure failed in all three of the Triple Crown classics, he was not dishonored by losing to such greats as Bold Forbes and, later, the great gelding Forego. Again, What a Pleasure led the nation both as best national stallion and national juvenile stallion by earnings.

Unfortunately, Howard Sams did not live to see his champions perform. When he died in 1974, son Tim sold the farm to Gilbert Campbell, who turned it into Stonehedge Farm, a major contributor to the industry in the '80s and '90s. A real estate developer in Massachusetts, Campbell entered the Florida Thoroughbred scene with this purchase.

In 1975, Fred Hooper won the national award for Breeder of the Year. Then, in 1976, Jack Dreyfuss of Hobeau Farm was awarded the very first ever Eclipse Award of Merit. Considered Thoroughbred racing's highest honor, this award is presented to an individual or entity displaying outstanding lifetime achievement in, and service to, the Thoroughbred industry. Horses assisting this awarding included Beau Purple, which defeated Kelso in the Man o' War Stakes at Belmont Park in October 1962; Onion, which defeated Secretariat in the Whitney Stakes in August 1973; Prove Out, which defeated Secretariat in the Woodward Stakes in September 1973; Handsome Boy, which defeated Buckpasser in the

Honest Pleasure. *Photo by Jim Jernigan.*

Brooklyn Handicap in July 1967; and Blessing Angelica, which won the Delaware Handicap in 1971 and 1972.

All of these successes added to the explosive nature of the industry in central Florida. In 1976, Bridlewood Farm was created from the ground up. It would produce more than one hundred stakes winners and dozens of graded stakes winners. Arthur Appleton of Appleton Electric Company and his wife, Martha, left not just an equine legacy but also an art collection accumulated during years of world traveling. The Appleton Museum, created in 1987, ensures that their name will never be forgotten in Marion County. He died in 2008, and Bridlewood Farm, long for sale, finally sold in 2013 for $14 million to billionaire John Malone, who made his fortune in the cable television industry. According to the *Ocala Star Banner*, Malone is the largest private landowner in America, the eight-hundred-acre farm in Florida a mere drop in his bucket. This is his first foray into the Thoroughbred industry. Only history will tell.

By the end of 1977, both Dr. Fager and In Reality topped the general and juvenile sire lists. Deceased Dr. Fager became the first Florida-bred to top the North American general sire list. While What a Pleasure topped the lists in 1975 and 1976, he was not a Florida-bred; Dr. Fager was the first Florida-bred to do so. He did it with progeny earnings of $1,593,079. In Reality was leading juvenile sire with progeny earnings of $432,596.

THIS WAS THE SPACE age; computers, fiber optics and video games were just being developed. Pocket calculators took away the need to learn math, while cassette tapes made music portable and microwave ovens made it easier for housewives to seek outside work. Keeping the attention of an increasingly fast-paced public took more than it had in the past. Racing had serious competition with the incoming age of technology. The magical Secretariat had stimulated an enormous amount of interest for a time. When Seattle Slew also claimed the Triple Crown only four years later, it seemed almost easy. It was the only award still unclaimed by Florida.

Louis and Patrice Wolfson still dreamed of a Kentucky Derby winner. Harbor View Farm had a reputation for high-quality horses, but that Derby win still eluded them. Wolfson, who had raced Raise a Native and believed in that bloodline, chose one of his sons, Exclusive Native, to breed to a Crafty Admiral mare named Won't Tell You. The brilliant chestnut colt was foaled at Harbor View Farm on February 21, 1975. Patrice recalled fondly how Affirmed was a gentle and affectionate colt from the start, always easy to get along with. He would come to the fence and put his head in her arms, ignoring the antics of the other colts.

Ironically, a son of Raise a Native himself was born the same year at the famous and long-established Calumet Farm in Kentucky. Owner Lucille Wright had already captured four Kentucky Derbies and two Triple Crowns. It was in her blood, and at the end of her days, she wanted one more, probably her last.

Both colts showed talent from the beginning. Calumet's Alydar's workouts were so good that his trainer, John Veitch, had difficulty finding a maiden race for him; his workouts scared off the competition. Therefore, his first start was the Youthful Stakes at Belmont Park. He was green and finished fifth behind an equally green but unbeaten second-time starter, his "cousin," Florida-bred Affirmed. Calumet was not worried; it was certain that it had its next Derby winner.

In the Great American Stakes, Alydar put in a better showing, beating Affirmed, but then both colts went on to capture four more major races apart from each other. They next came together in the Champagne Stakes, where Alydar beat Affirmed by a length and a quarter. Affirmed came back to tag him by a neck in the Laurel Futurity. After six meetings in their juvenile year, the public was excited by the dueling duo.

In the fall of 1977, just months before Affirmed would begin his historic run at the Triple Crown, the Wolfsons dissolved Harbor View, selling off most of the property to their sons, Stephen and Gary, who owned nearby Happy Valley Farm and were running up successes of their own.

By the end of 1977, both talented colts were in the running for Champion 2-Year-Old Colt of the Year. But while Alydar had suffered a loss to another horse, Affirmed's only losses were to Alydar. He had a record of five wins in seven starts to Alydar's five wins in ten starts. Affirmed took the championship honors, with Alydar runner-up. The stage was set for their classic year.

Laz Barrera, Affirmed's trainer, took his colt to California to prep for the classics; interestingly, Alydar, the Kentucky-bred, was sent to Florida. Alydar tuned up with a talented In Reality colt named Believe It, while Affirmed was forced to walk the shedrows due to an unusual monsoon season that kept the tracks too wet to risk a valuable horse.

Both horses had cakewalks in their first allowance starts of the new year. Affirmed followed that with the San Felipe Handicap, where new and upcoming rider Steve Cauthen had to remind Affirmed of his duty, not because he risked losing but because the bright chestnut liked to flick his ears as he listened to the crowds, look up at the birds or check out the "labored breathing of his pursuers," according to the *Blood Horse* book *The 10 Best Kentucky Derbies*. Throughout his career, Affirmed would coast in a relaxed, unhurried way when on the lead but dig in competitively the moment anyone ranged alongside. As long as he won, distance away didn't seem to matter.

The Santa Anita Derby, the best California had to offer, was equally easy for the big colt. Affirmed led the entire way to an eight-length victory. Some critics began to wonder if the colt was a little too relaxed in his racing style. He claimed one more stakes, the Hollywood Derby, and then his hooves were set on the road to Kentucky. Alydar had similar easy wins in the Flamingo and then the Florida Derby, although in the latter, he was hard-pressed again by Believe It.

Back in Kentucky for the final prep race, the Blue Grass Stakes, Admiral and Mrs. Gene Markey (Lucille Wright of Calumet) were given the grand entrance of being driven to the track and seated right at the finish line. Affirmed's trainer chose not to risk his horse in this race, only nine days before the Derby, so Alydar sported an easy, thirteen-length victory, after which jockey Jorge Velasquez took Alydar to the rail so that the grande dame could pet her baby.

Laz Barrera kept hearing that his horse couldn't win because he was a Florida-bred and had been racing in California. Woody Stephens, trainer of Believe It, was quoted in *The Florida Horse* by Jim Bolus, "I don't think California horses compare with these kinds of horses. There have been a couple of horses come out of California and win the Derby but more horses come out of Gulfstream and Hialeah." Barrera wasn't worried. He told reporters that Affirmed slept in the mornings of races, while all the other horses got hyper. He'd be ready for the first Saturday in May.

Four days before the Derby, Wolfson and his wife, Patrice, met with reporters on the backside of Churchill Downs. Wolfson predicted, "If Affirmed is in front at the top of the stretch, you can put your binoculars down, because Alydar won't catch him." He explained that after examining the six earlier meetings between the two as 2-year-olds, it seemed to him that Affirmed really dug in when things get toughest. Both had won all their starts in their 3-year-old year, without yet meeting each other.

After both of these remarkable horses had proven this year's Derby likely to be a two-horse race, still nine other candidates showed up to vie for third place. Both horses were brilliant chestnuts, massive, gorgeous racing machines, with Alydar slightly the heavier and taller. Much Kentucky sentiment rode with this horse to the gate, but Florida, too, had a strong contingent in the stands.

Racing management was ecstatic; it had been 1973 since such a large crowd showed up for Secretariat's Derby. They watched the black and pink silks of Harbor View and the devil's red and blue of Calumet enter the track at Churchill Downs atop two brilliant chestnuts. Hometown sentimentality sent Alydar off as favorite.

Affirmed broke into a comfortable third position, while Alydar broke and retreated for reasons no one could understand. It was not his usual running manner. By the quarter pole, Affirmed had an easy lead, but Alydar was finally pounding up from behind, still not close enough for the leaders to know where he was. When Believe It made a run for Affirmed, everyone's pace quickened. But the plucky Believe It could only hang on for third as Alydar charged past for second, a length and a half behind Affirmed, to the everlasting disappointment of the Kentuckians.

No one knew why Alydar had been so slow to rouse, but he acquitted himself far better in the second two legs of the Triple Crown. In both, the two dueled in highly dramatic fashion. After running the fifth-fastest Derby, now they ran the second-fastest Preakness, tying with Secretariat's time, Alydar a mere neck behind Affirmed. Only five horses chose to contest

Affirmed at Belmont. *Photo by NYRA.*

the Belmont with the duo. Everyone's hearts were in their throats as they watched the two toss the lead back and forth, the finish never certain, even to the end. The two courageous campaigners hit the wire in a photo finish. But soon the announcement came: the Florida industry had won the last accolade left to it, the Triple Crown!

In the *Blood Horse* of April 26, 2008, on the thirty-year anniversary of the famed Derby, Dan Liebman wrote that Affirmed's rider, Steve Cauthen, said, "The longest three weeks of my life were in between the Preakness and the Belmont. There wasn't a lot between those two horses; one small mistake, one little thing, could switch it going either way."

In the *Sports Illustrated* of June 19, 1978, William Leggett wrote, "Nothing between Affirmed and Alydar has ever been easy. Their rivalry is so intense, so close that it transcends what is supposedly racing's best show, the Triple Crown. Years from now people will not only recall that Affirmed earned the toughest Triple Crown ever contested but that Alydar was the first horse to run second in all three legs."

Affirmed became the eleventh Triple Crown winner, and eleven it remains still, as of 2014. Perhaps the greatest significance of the Affirmed story is that no one has been able to duplicate it. Once and for all, a Florida-bred had proven that it could compete in the best and against the best.

The only time the two ever met again, Affirmed won again but was disqualified for having lurched in front of Alydar. The final tally was Affirmed seven, Alydar three. Later that year, Affirmed met 1977 Triple Crown winner

Affirmed. *Painting by Angie Draper.*

Seattle Slew, the first time two Triple Crown winners ever came together. A speedball, Seattle Slew flew to the lead and never let Affirmed near. The only other time they met, Affirmed's saddle slipped so that his jockey was forced to just hang on, and again Seattle Slew won. These unfortunate losses were the reason for Affirmed missing 1978 Horse of the Year.

Nonetheless, by the end of that extraordinary year, Affirmed had claimed the Champion 3-Year-Old Colt honors, while other Florida-breds MacDiarmida, Dr. Patches and It's in the Air took, respectively, Champion Turf Horse, Champion Sprinter and Champion 2-Year-Old Filly (with It's In the Air bred by Happy Valley Farm but raced by the older Wolfsons). Harbor View Farm won the Eclipse Awards for Outstanding Breeder and Owner of the Year.

The farm would continue to lead the nation as Leading Owner by Money Won in 1979 and 1980 because Affirmed was not done. The following year, he came back to win six consecutive Grade 1 stakes races (TOBA instituted a grading system in 1973, Grade 1 being the highest quality of stakes worldwide), set a track record and beat Kentucky Derby and Preakness winner Spectacular Bid in a match race. By the end of the year, he had become the first horse to beat Kelso's record by becoming the Thoroughbred world's highest earner ever with $2,393,818 to his credit. He was named Champion Handicap Horse and Horse of the Year at last.

Chapter 8

HORSE CAPITAL OF THE WORLD

In 1982, census takers listed Ocala as the second-fastest-growing metropolitan area in the United States (second only to Fort Myers, Florida). The rapid growth could easily be laid at the feet of the equally fast-growing Thoroughbred industry. The late 1970s and the early 1980s were the heyday of racing and breeding of Thoroughbred racehorses everywhere. The world's richest men, like Robert Sangster of the Isle of Man; Nelson Bunker Hunt, the silver magnate; Arab sheiks; and many others arrived annually at the premier sales of Thoroughbred stock, the Keenelend and the Saratoga Yearling Sales, to purchase the best blood money could buy, often taking the young stock back to their own countries. The price of a horse, any horse, was driven higher and higher.

Many of these wealthiest people the world had to offer also boarded or bought farms in the United States, where the tax laws were so favorable. Racehorse investors could write off their equine losses against other businesses. The tiny Ocala airport had to be lengthened to accommodate the private jets flying in from all over the world. Everyone made money; it was a highly energized and enthusiastic time. The sales were great parties where one could rub elbows at the bars or the sales ring with wealthy people from all over the world.

Women flirted, men boasted and everyone gambled. Dressed in heels, pearls and diamonds or jeans, boots and a cowboy hat, it didn't matter. It was a fun and exciting time to be in the business of racehorses. Summering at Saratoga and wintering at Hialeah was not just the good old days—it was

Signposts on the corner in 2013. *Photos by Charlene R. Johnson.*

Bridlewood Junction in 1982. Those who came to the big parties hosted at the farm were treated to an electric train ride around the lavish property. *Photo by Charlene R. Johnson.*

now. It was the glory days of the "Sport of Kings," and many not so kingly went along for the ride. It was during this time that the greatest sire of the twentieth century, Northern Dancer, standing in Maryland, demanded the highest stud fee ever in the history of the industry: $1 million. In 1983, one of his yearlings sold at the Keeneland sale for $10 million, while in 1984, twelve of his yearlings sold for an unprecedented average of $3,446,666.

New agents and agencies sprouted; syndications were put together in minutes at the side of the sales ring. Pinhooking, the purchase of a horse to flip-flop back to the sales in a short time, sprang into the lingo of the turf.

In the spring of 1979, Dan Lasater contacted Kenneth Noe Jr., general manager of Calder Race Course, to discuss the idea of a new racing series to showcase the offspring of his impressive roster of stallions. However, although Kenny Noe liked the idea, he didn't want a private series, so he contacted then president of the FTBA Fred Hooper, who got Florida breeding columnist Chuck Tilley and trainer John Nerud of Tartan involved. They created a new race series to showcase all of Florida's stallions.

Any stallion owner who wanted to be involved nominated his stallion for $2,500 in 1979. Those stallions' as yet unborn foals were then eligible to run as 2-year-olds in the series at Calder in 1982. Graduated payments would continue to be made by the foal owners to keep the foals eligible up to the day of the race. If sold before then, the new owners picked up the payments. Being eligible, however, raised the value of both stallions and foals.

The first series was held in 1982. Hoping originally for 75 stallions, the creators were delighted with 101 stallions nominated, resulting in 400 eligible juveniles and total purses of $856,500. The races were all named in honor of the greatest Florida-breds to date: the Dr. Fager division was competed at six furlongs; the Desert Vixen division for the fillies at six; the Affirmed division held at seven furlongs; the Susan's Girl division the fillies' counterpart; and the In Reality division one and a sixteenth miles, while the My Dear Girl division was for the fillies at the same distance. These races were held a pair at a time several weeks apart so that the same animals could compete at the growing distances as they matured, thus making possible a sweep of the entire series. By 2012, only 11 horses had won all three of their series, while 36 horses had won two of the three. Although the series was not limited to Florida-breds, by 2012, only three horses not bred in the state had won.

The historic first running of the most unique state-bred program ever invented took off with Dan Lasater's stallions indeed scoring well when Crystal Rail by his Great Above and out of Susan's Girl won the filly division, and El Kaiser by his Raise a Bid won the colt division. So popular was this series that many times over the years, divisions have had to be split to accommodate the high numbers of entries. Ten years later, Calder management conceived of combining the finale of the two distance races, which had been held a week apart, with a whole day of high-quality stakes and family entertainment. They named this day the "Festival of the Sun." It sports the richest races of the year in the state for 2-year-olds.

To this day, it remains the most popular and profitable state series ever devised. The series has shown to be a great proving ground for young racehorses; many of the winners go on to make big names for themselves nationally. Other states began to emulate with series of their own.

In 2011, the FTBOA assumed the program from Calder and began collecting the stallion registrations in 2011 and 2012. (On May 5, 1993, "Owners" was added to the FTBA name, now officially listed as FTBA, dba FTBOA. This was a recognition that owners are as important a part of the industry as breeders.) The year 2013 was the last time Calder administered the series. From here on, the FTBOA will take over and expand on the series, renaming it the "Florida Sire Stakes Program" and including 3-year-old races. Although the Florida Stallion Stakes program is incorporated into it, it is now designed for FTBOA-registered horses only. It anticipates more than $2.2 million in purses. It will no longer be limited to Calder but rather will also be run at Gulfstream Park and Tampa Bay Downs.

One result of this series was inspiration for the creation of the Breeders' Cup series, the richest series of races in the world. Nerud and Hooper partnered with Kentuckian John Gaines and others to create this most prestigious series of races to date. From the first, Florida-breds have won their share in this series as well. It is considered one of the richest days in sports in the world.

In 1983, Florida-breds raced so well that they depleted the breeders' awards pot. The fund went into the hole by some $300,000. When a single breeder of successful racehorses who also owned the stallion pocketed a $90,000 check, the FTBA decided that it was time to restructure. Senate Bill #777 put the breeders' pot directly under the control of the FTBA, nicely eliminating the state's surcharge of 6 percent just to handle the money. It was a more finite pot, however, so the FTBA was allowed to set a cap. No more $90,000 checks! The same year, it passed the right to issue owners' awards for the first time as well as breeders' awards.

It was clear that stallions were making it as big in the Sunshine State as the racehorses. But from the beginning of the Thoroughbred industry in Florida, it would take serious thought to keep a big-name stallion in Florida. No matter how you cut it, that dangling peninsula in the middle of the ocean was just a long way away from the other breeding centers. Besides costing money to ship distances, valuable mares were always at risk when shipped. Although local breeders were hailed as heroes every time they brought or kept a good stallion in the state, and although there is no doubt that it helped

Mr. Prospector in 1981. *Photo by Charlene R. Johnson.*

the pedigrees of Florida-breds, there was never any doubt that more money could be made if said stallion held court in Kentucky instead.

One of the best stallions to be created in Florida was Mr. Prospector. A Kentucky-bred son of Raise a Native (which always did well with Sunshine

143

blood) out of a Nashua mare, Mr. P was a $200,000 yearling in 1971 when that was considered steep. While he proved a good sprinter, it was not his race record that would ultimately make headlines but rather his stud record. His speed fit Florida bloodlines well, and he quickly proved himself a great sire.

It seemed that, when bred to a distance mare, his speed combined with her talent and resulted in sheer genius. Savin was approached by Bluegrass breeders, and Florida simply could not compete. The successes of Gold Beauty and Conquistador Cielo the very year Mr. P moved to Kentucky only proved the Kentuckians right for stealing and the Floridians right for complaining.

Gold Beauty was named Champion Sprinter of 1982. Conquistador Cielo, who was pure poetry in motion, captured Horse of the Year and Champion 3-Year-Old Colt the same year. His win was by a single tie-breaking vote, the closest in the history of the awards. The three voting organizations—*Daily Racing Form*, Thoroughbred Racing Association and National Turf Writers' Association—selected three different horses for Horse of the Year. Only by awarding points for second and third did Conquistador Cielo beat out Landaluce and Lemhi Gold. However, he was unanimous choice for 3-Year-Old Colt, with Florida-breds running second and third as well. By the time he retired from racing to the stud barns in Kentucky, he was syndicated for a then record price of $36.4 million.

His foals went on to command record sales prices and continued to prove themselves at the races. Mr. Prospector, called "Sire of Sires," would sire Fappiano, who would sire Unbridled among many others. Mr. Prospector would be compared to Northern Dancer as two of the best stallions ever produced in America.

While this sucking away of the best blood was an emotional struggle and led to some bitterness in the early years, by 2013, most breeders philosophically contended that Florida had shown itself a proving ground for a young stallion; however, as fast as the proven ones are stolen away, new ones take their place. In such a way, Florida has often been the first to have the best of recently retired stallions. It is now considered a compliment and just part of doing business in Florida.

One indicator of the volcanic growth of the equine business in central Florida was the proliferation of premier veterinary facilities and other services. When Dr. Reuben Brawner arrived in 1944 as the third licensed vet in the county, and making $200 per month, he became enamored of the burgeoning equine industry. It was he who helped Madeline Leach with

Conquistador Cielo on the backside of Saratoga Race Course. *Photo by Charlene R. Johnson.*

a sickly foal named Needles. He soon began specializing in equines when such a thing was virtually unheard of. He can be rightfully credited with supporting the equine industry through its formative years. He was much beloved and respected in the community throughout his forty-five years of doing business and long after retirement. Diane Dudley Parks remembered him well. "Dr. Brawner used to work out of the trunk of the car and drove himself. Today the vets have drivers, a computer in the front seat and a big old Suburban with everything you need in it."

Drs. William L. Lyall and Manulani Lyall opened up what was slated to be the most modern equine hospital in the country in the 1960s. They were attracted to Ocala from Kentucky because of the huge growth spurt and the need for such facilities. They provided some surgery and hydraulic operating tables. As of 2013, a church sits on the Lyall property.

In 1976, spurred by central Florida's exploding equine growth, the University of Florida in Gainesville created the School of Veterinary Medicine and turned out its first graduating class in 1980. A state act forming a partnership between land-grant universities and the U.S. Department of Agriculture created extension vets who work out of the colleges. Every county has an extension office, staffed by agents who specialize in what is important in the area. In central Florida, that would be equine. By 2001, UF ranked among the top ten veterinary schools in the nation, and it was aiming at the top five. Its strong equine program was attributed directly to the Marion County equine population.

When Dr. John L. Peterson, who had started with the Lyalls, opened his state-of-the-art, ten-thousand-square-foot hospital, complete with surgical facilities in 1982, he hired surgeon Dr. Don E. Slone, one of only fifty-five board-certified equine surgeons in the United States, of whom only about fifteen were in private practice. Most were associated with universities. UF, which had been fighting personnel, time and facility shortages, with an eight-week waiting list for elective surgery, was grateful and supportive of the new facility. In the 2000s, equine vets and hospitals are too numerous to count.

Alternative services like Reiki, acupuncture and massage for horses also had a strong following by 2013. Feed stores mimicked the veterinarians. In the beginning, for years, there was only the Seminole Feed Store. Now there's Seminole, Berettini, Midwest, Ocala Breeders' Sales Company (OBS) and all kinds of other feed stores.

The sales also reflected the growth. In 1974, after leading FBSC for sixteen years, O'Farrell had a falling out with the company and helped form the Ocala Breeders' Sales Company as a cooperative organization, a rival company. OBS broke ground for a new $1.6 million facility, while in reaction, FBSC announced extensive improvements to its Southeastern Livestock Pavilion. OBS finished its new facility west of Ocala across from the airport in record time and, in January 1975, held its first sale in the state-of-the-art facility. Once again, Ocala Stud was the largest consignor. Meanwhile, this was the eighteenth year of the Hialeah sales, where this time the largest consignor was Farnsworth Farms. At first, OBS held only breeding stock sales, leaving the 2-year-old sales to FBSC in the south.

OBS quickly became the premier place to sell breeding stock, so in 1980, George Steinbrenner purchased FBSC rather than allow a merger of OBS and FBSC, but it turned out to be a mere delay. By 1984, the Ocala Breeders' Sales Company bought out Florida Breeders' Sales Company, which not only ended a historic era but also set OBS on the road to becoming the biggest seller of Thoroughbred stock in the United States. It then began holding 2-year-old sales in Ocala. This facility has grown over the years to include an off-track betting site, and it continues to be the scene of some of the most successful horse sales in the country. In 2013, it hosted the largest and most successful 2-year-old sales anywhere in the United States. OBS handles about 60 percent of the 2-year-old market nationwide.

Tom Ventura, president of OBS in 2014, has watched the changes over the last thirty years:

The 2-year-old sales have changed significantly. When we first started, they galloped down the lanes, usually in pairs with exercise riders from the farms, and it showed the horse's movement. Then it progressed, and we started breezing them, getting lighter and more professional riders rather than people from the farms. [In the old days] the buyers may or may not have been there for the workouts; they would pick up the timesheets when they came to the sale. Then it advanced to the videos. That was great for the buyers, but now the sellers had to put on a better show, avoid whipping, etc. Now time and movement could be scrutinized over and over.

We used to ship those bulky VHS tapes out well in advance of the sale. Then we went to DVDs and were also able to stream, which is where we are currently. The workouts and the sale are streamed live so that wherever you are in the world, you can watch the entire show. Editing technology is better, and it all gets posted to the website faster. DVDs are becoming less important. People stand at the sales ring with iPads in hand now, or they can go to touchscreen kiosks and press buttons to see the workouts, even watch the sale indoors while they're out in the ring.

The 2-year-old sales were first invented to showcase horses that didn't have much in pedigree. Very innovative at the time, but now pinhookers are buying, breaking and training, and we have tremendous success stories running through our sales. So now we are a true source for finding a great horse both by performance and pedigree. Those are the two biggest changes in the 2-year-old sales over the years.

On December 30, 1982, Joseph Michael O'Farrell died. Hailed as the "granddaddy of the Florida thoroughbred industry" by the local television station and a "vital cog in the growth of Florida's thoroughbred industry" by *The Florida Horse* magazine, the *Ocala Star Banner* wrote of him, "He shares much of the responsibility of putting Florida on the map as a horse breeding state. Not just the thoroughbred industry but Ocala, Marion County and all of Florida lost a great asset in the death of Joe O'Farrell."

O'Farrell died at seventy doing what he loved best, what he had turned into an art form: inspecting his 2-year-olds in training for the upcoming sales. Among the thousands who mourned him, there was much speculation on what Marion County would have been like had he never settled here. What he and Rose, Heath, Dudley, Price and a few other pioneers did, with the assistance of a few courageous horses, changed the course of history, not just for Marion County but for all of Florida.

His friend Bonnie Heath said, "Joe was always the driving force, very dramatic. He just knew that Ocala could become what it is today. He had unbridled confidence in the industry here."

In a memorial to him in *The Florida Horse* of February 1983, the FBSC wrote, "We thank him for his foresight and courage in conducting the first Florida sales, which were the basis of today's multi-million dollar industry… We acknowledge that he had a profound influence on the success of the Florida thoroughbred industry, thereby touching the lives of many who never had the privilege of knowing him."

Like Carl Rose before him, Joseph O'Farrell died doubtless deeply satisfied at seeing his beloved Ocala Stud, Marion County and Florida on top of the breeding and racing world. He could die feeling that he had succeeded at his greatest passion. No single person in the industry would ever again have such direct impact, but then it wouldn't be needed. The pioneers had done their jobs well.

THE TIMING WAS PERFECT for Joe; he did not live to see the crash. The words of the "Fast Horses of Marion County" website sum up the industry well: "Breeding race horses in Ocala has a rich history. It started slow, gained speed, produced world champions, stumbled badly, and recovered." To that quote could be added, "…stumbled badly again and recovered again."

Inflation never works; when things fly unrealistically high, they only have much farther to fall. A few things contributed to the sudden collapse within the industry in the late 1980s. When the folks from other countries had purchased enough fine-blooded stock to begin breeding their own animals, they no longer needed American bloodlines. But perhaps the most devastating cause was that in 1986, federal tax laws allowing racehorses to be tax write-offs were repealed. The racehorse business could no longer provide shelters for other businesses. Investors, foreign and American, withdrew; the wealthy scrambled to find other outlets. Seemingly overnight, those high stud fees for foals still in the belly were not possible to recoup. Sales prices plummeted. Whole farms and many individuals lost everything in all of the equine centers, from Kentucky to California, Maryland, New York and Florida. Finally on equal footing, everyone plummeted. Almost overnight "horsemen" found themselves with bad horses worth nothing and good horses worth far less than anticipated. Breeders, whose return is long term, found it very difficult to recover. Many were knocked out of the game completely.

Economist Peter Karunga explained it in his abstract *Macroeconomic Factors and the Thoroughbred Industry*:

Thoroughbreds are capital assets whose values stem from expected future net returns from racing and breeding. Many Thoroughbreds, especially yearlings, are sold at auctions which bring together foreign and domestic breeders. Thus, macroeconomic factors should play a major role in determining the health of the industry.

In the mid-1980s, the thoroughbred industry experienced an unprecedented economic boom. Foreign breeders invested heavily in American-bred yearlings and this boosted prices to historically high levels, especially at the major thoroughbred sale sites where foreigners purchase horses—Keeneland (Lexington, KY) and Saratoga (Saratoga, NY) sales. However, since 1985, the industry has undergone significant economic decline. In 1984, the average price of a selected yearling from the combined Keeneland and Saratoga summer sales was slightly over $456,000 compared to an average of slightly over $294,982 for 1990.

This research paper went on to test the hypothesis that both exchange rates and interest rates affect the price of Thoroughbred yearlings. From 1980 to 1982, the exchange rate rose by 20 percent, which caused the real value of U.S. exports like corn and wheat to decline by three-fourths.

The equine industry in the U.S., with over 5.25 million horses and 32 states participating in horse racing is a multi-billion industry contributing over $15 billion annually to the gross domestic product. Between 1975 and 1988 the industry contributed an average $600 million to the Federal government from its pari-mutuel wagering activities. By 1988, 32 states had about 100 race tracks and a total attendance of about 69 million… which contributes significantly to the economics of many states.

Between 1981 and 1990, 35% of the total yearlings auctioned at Keeneland and Saratoga were purchased by foreign investors, accounting for 53% of the total gross expenditure on yearling sales…foreign buyers tend to buy higher-priced yearlings.

The 1986 Tax Reform Act affected the industry in three fundamental ways: 1) The Passive Activity Loss—before this, the industry benefitted from capital infusions by people who needed to shelter large sums of money and these investments in the industry were tax-exempt. This act stopped this.

Newberry argues that there is no change in the Internal Revenue Code which has had such a profound impact on the thoroughbred industry as the passive loss provision. 2) Income tax from horses classified as capital assets (mainly broodmares and stallions) rose from 20% to 28%. 3) the Act lowered the depreciation rate for the industry.

The results of this study were the conclusions that a major factor which helped yearling prices increase in the early 1980s (the exchange rate) turned against the yearling market in the late 1980s. The tax law change was the other serious price reducing event.

The effect of the exchange rate on the thoroughbred industry enhances our understanding of its effect on a specific commodity or product. The yearling market presents a unique opportunity to study the impacts of an exchange rate change because of the obvious presence of foreign buyers at the auction. If a product relies heavily on foreign markets, the exchange rate can play a major role in product demand and price.

Where the industry was concentrated, like central Florida, the trickle-down affected everything—farms went bankrupt, and jobs disappeared. Just in Marion County, the production of foals had dropped from 5,000 to less than 2,500 by 1987. While many folks and farms disappeared and everyone took a hit, the knowledgeable horse person was most likely to survive. As the industry slowly began to recover, it took on a new look. Those who had survived and new ones coming in began to build a stronger base. The wealthy would still participate, but now the regular guy or gal had more of a chance. Large farms were cut into smaller farms; one- and two-horse farms were born. Marion County would never again sport the huge farms that once dominated the local industry.

One of the new things that began to happen was an increase in pinhooking. Horsemanship now counted for much more than how much money one spent on a horse. While the breeder must invest long term—a stud fee, care of the gestating mare, the trauma of birth and then raising a healthy foal, hoping all goes well—the pinhooker takes advantage of the breeder going through all that and then purchases a live, certifiably healthy animal.

Representative of this new trend are Nick and Jaqui deMeric. They began pinhooking in the early 1980s, when it was still an unusual thing to do. Nick and Jaqui both had been horse crazy all their lives, so when they met in Kentucky working for the same sales agent in 1981, it was a natural match. They quickly decided to make Marion County their base and slowly began to grow a business.

They leased one stall and free-lanced for other people as riders, squirreling away their dollars as they earned them. They purchased their first horse together and, in March 1983, sold her for a small profit, which then enabled them to buy a reliable vehicle and get married. "If I'd known then how much was riding on that one horse," Nick laughed in 2013, "I'd have been a lot more nervous about that sale! If that horse had gone belly up we might still be free-lancing for other people!"

The following year, they were able to rent a whole barn and eighty acres and use the racetrack on Stavola Farm. Several years and several pinhooked horses later—along with a few loyal clients, partnerships and work as agents—they purchased their first forty acres. "Back then, very few people pinhooked," Nick said. "But for us, it combined the best of both worlds. We didn't have the money to buy a big farm and start right in breeding top horses, and we didn't want to raise a family running around the racetracks. So pinhooking, while it was always a risky gamble, gave us the opportunity to get ahead, create a home and raise a family in a rural environment."

Their first major pinhooking success was a filly purchased for $43,000 as a yearling. They sent her back through the sales and took home $280,000. Their operation expanded in size until, by 1997, they had added a 230-acre chunk of land that became the Eclipse Training Center. Along the way, they managed to raise a son and daughter who as grown-ups are also engaged in the industry.

DeMeric continued:

> We have to be better about picking the individuals we choose. That bar gets higher and higher when people are worried about their money and the economy is tight. I remember very well that horrible first year after the crash. We didn't even sell half of the horses we put up in Miami, but in the process we learned damage control. We made videos when that was still pretty rare and pushed one horse at a time and came out of it all right. The result of making adjustments was a better year following.
>
> That said, 1986 was like falling off a cliff; everyone felt that one. One advantage of pinhooking is that we are working on an annual cycle as opposed to long-term, which means that you do have the opportunity to regroup, which the owner of a broodmare band doesn't have. They have to go the full cycle of the foals in belly, weanlings in field, yearlings prepping for a sale, and so they are usually harder hit, unless they are that higher end.

Many can tell a similar tale. Following the triage of the 1980s, it is good horsemen and horsewomen like these who have turned pinhooking into an art form and put a new face on the industry. People with a dream and a knowledge of horses found it possible to pursue their dream, slowly at first, but with discipline, frugality and passion, they helped create the new industry of the 1990s and the 2000s. They were a better breed of horsemen and women; they had to be. By the 2000s, pinhooking had gained so much in popularity that there are more pinhookers than breeders buying and selling horses through the sales. Although painful at the time, looking back, most would agree that it was good for the industry. The crash of the 1980s was a leveling field for everyone, Kentuckian, Marylander and Floridian alike. Today, the Florida pinhooker buys a top-class yearling at the top yearling sales like anyone else. Boundaries are far less finite.

While this explosion in pinhooking and opportunities for new people is one side of the coin, Michael O'Farrell sees the other side:

> We used to have forty breeding farms breeding to sell as 2-year-olds. When the pinhookers got involved, a lot of them didn't have money at first so they might borrow money, and they bought $15,000 and $20,000 horses to train and sell at the 2-year-old sales. We local breeders were able to compete with them at that point because they were buying good-looking horses that didn't have much pedigree, inexpensive horses.
>
> Well, now that's all changed. Some of them made money, some borrowed more, some got investors, even Kentucky breeders funneling horses to them. So now in today's world, you have to get 2-year olds that can compete with the best bloodlines out there. They won't be dogs. Now these pinhookers can pay $150,000 to half a million for a yearling to sell at the 2-year-old sale. Pinhookers have gotten to be very good at what they do. Today, we have very good horsemen who are working people, and it's very competitive. They aren't made of money, and they're bidding against each other on the same yearling. They can buy good horses; they can go to the Keeneland yearling sale in September and compete with the big boys. If they see an athlete, they'll pay the $150,000 or more and hope to get $400,000 at the 2-year-old sale, and it works for them. They can pick and choose what they want to take to a sale. Me as a breeder, I can't pick and choose. I still have to deal with what the good Lord gives me. It's tough when you have to compete, but that's what it is.

The triage also opened the door of opportunity for others who might not have gotten a foot through as quickly. A longtime commodity of the racetracks were the Hispanic exercise riders and jockeys—Mexicans, Venezuelans, Argentinians, Brazilians and many others. Often smaller than their Caucasian counterparts but strong, and perhaps with an inherent understanding of the equine, when they showed talent in their own countries, they were often imported by owners or trainers to work America's tracks.

But by the 1990s, they had begun appearing on the farms in ever-growing numbers, not just in Florida but in all the Thoroughbred communities. Their families often followed once they proved themselves valuable workers. The people working DeMeric's farms are now second generation. "Our employees are like family," he said. "They've been with us for a lot of years. We host Thanksgiving for everyone every year, and we have over one hundred people with all their munchkins running around."

In the 2000s, Hispanic horsemen and women are not just farm help; many have gone on, through persistence and hard work, to pinhooking and creating their own successful farms and training centers.

Nearly everyone credited Hispanics with being the hardest workers in the industry these days. Horsemen who prefer to remain anonymous agreed: "The minute they get their hands on a little money, they save it up, they're buying a horse, galloping it themselves and selling it themselves. Some of them have made enormous amounts of money."

Wealthy Venezuelans and other South Americans have also purchased farms of their own. South America has become very bullish on farms in the last few years. A knowledge of Spanish is a useful skill on today's equine farms. Although the central Florida industry still sports some large, beautiful, clearly well-backed farms, most of the "new" horseman are hands-on and live in the area, as opposed to the many wealthy landowners of yesteryear who stopped by their farms periodically.

SILVER CHARM IS INDICATIVE of the "new" Thoroughbred industry. "The Charm," as he came to be called, was bred by Mary Lou Wootten, who admitted that she and her husband, Gordon, were small players in a big game. They bred Silver Charm from a mare they claimed at Aqueduct for $16,500. They sold the mare, before her son's racing career got started, for a mere $4,200 at the October Mixed Sale. They maintained a band of only three broodmares, and they love and support the industry to the best of their ability.

The gray colt by Silver Buck was foaled and raised to a yearling at Scott and Diane Dudley's Dudley Farm. Jack Dudley, who died on October 18, 1998, was still alive to see the handsome gray colt romping in the fields and to witness his early races. They turned the yearling colt over to a new agent, Janie Roper, who had gotten her start as an exercise rider at the Dudley Farm and was just starting her own business. She entered him in the OBS August yearling sale in 1995, and he sold for $16,500.

He was purchased by professional pinhookers Randy Hartley and Dean de Renzo, who broke and trained him at their Hartley DeRenzo Thoroughbreds facility north of Ocala. Their website notes, "The Florida based company began as a pinhooking operation and has evolved into a full service breeding, training and sales facility," again, a representation of what much of the central Florida industry has become.

The Charm began to show promise as he progressed with his education. Failing the pedigree standards of the select sales, he had to wait for the April 2-year-old in training sales. When he clipped off the fastest breeze of the sale for a quarter mile (:21 4/5), he was suddenly the focus of much attention. Among those wowed by his workout were agents Kevin and J.B. McKathan, who had never purchased a 2-year-old before. But they wanted this one. They called trainer Bob Baffert, who agreed to bid after seeing a videotape of the workout, but the tape arrived too late and he missed the bidding. The colt was bought back for $100,000. The McKathans suggested a quick offer of $85,000 before other buyers could make offers, and so, on behalf of racing owners Robert and Beverly Lewis, Baffert agreed. The colt was purchased and taken to the McKathan Brothers Farm to be let down

Silver Charm at the Preakness. *Courtesy* The Florida Horse.

from his presale conditioning for a month. By the time he was shipped to California, to his new trainer and owners, he carried with him the hopes of many people and farms of central Florida.

Silver Charm won both the Kentucky Derby and the Preakness in 1997 in strongly battled photo finishes. Florida breeders were sure that they would see the next Triple Crown winner. He missed by a mere length when he ran second to Touch Gold in the Belmont. He was named Champion 3-Year-Old Colt of 1997. By the time Silver Charm retired sound to Three Chimneys Farm in Kentucky as a 5-year-old, he was the third-biggest money winner ever with $6,944,369, (behind another Florida-bred, Skip Away, at $9,616,360). Many thought that his Sunshine blood would provide a good outcross for the bluebloods. He was to stand for $25,000. Along this path, he had affected many lives. "He really helped jump-start a flagging industry," Diane Dudley Parks said. Florida, and the industry, had come a long way from its beginnings, as well as a long way from Roman Brother, the first colt ever to become a champion to have gone through a public auction.

EPILOGUE

As new people, horses and farms began to show up and the face of the industry changed to new ideas and new ways of doing business, so the old ones began to fade away. In 1990, Mrs. Frances Genter was named Breeder of the Year, helped out by Unbridled, Florida's fifth Kentucky Derby winner and Champion 3-Year-Old Colt. Both because of his owner—everyone loved Mrs. Genter—and because Unbridled was from Tartan Farms' last full crop, there was much sentimentality attached to this horse. Mrs. Genter paid $70,000 for him as a weanling in the Fasig-Tipton Kentucky sale in 1987. He would bag $4.5 million by the end of his career.

In January 1991, Bonnie M. Heath II stepped back and leased his 440-acre farm to his son, Bonnie M. Heath III, and daughter-in-law, Kim. Holy Bull, future Horse of the Year in 1994, slipped into Kim's arms and into the world five nights later, propelling them straight into a string of successes.

Many of the historic farms have long since fallen to the developer's blade—Paddock Mall, Central Florida College, roads and condominiums now stand where showplace farms worth millions once stood.

That engine driving the industry underwent dramatic changes as well. Racing nationwide saw a huge degeneration through the late 1990s and into the 2000s. Technology and entertainment have changed so much in the last decade or more that going to a racetrack just to watch a few horses run around an oval is, apparently, outdated. Nationwide, tracks that had proliferated through the 1970s and 1980s have gradually been purchased and consolidated by other track ownerships, died or have been turned into entertainment centers and casinos.

Hialeah Park Race Track was one of these. The only track ever to be listed on the National Register of Historic Places and an Audubon Bird Sanctuary, it nearly died several times, but it came back every time, sometimes with help from the state legislature. Even without its help, such as in 1972, when the state regulators declared Hialeah's traditional monopoly on the winter dates unconstitutional, it survived. But in 1987, the State of Florida entirely deregulated dates, and Hialeah never raced the coveted best winter dates again. Instead, Calder and Gulfstream fight over them. From the day of its first "legal" opening on January 14, 1932, Hialeah had been the shrine to racing, with Widener's vision patterned after the loveliest of Europe: Longchamp, Chantilly, Deauville and Ascot. Long labeled the "World's Most Beautiful Race Course," still, its attendance and handle dwindled, and despite leasing the facility for things like weddings and carnivals, the track hadn't made a profit since 1989. In 2001, it gave up the fight. "Many still can't get over the fact that it's closed," said Lonny Powell, CEO of the FTBOA since 2012. "Too bad for those who never got to see it."

Powell believes that the expansion of gambling has affected racing, and therefore breeding, more than anything else:

> There's just a lot more competition for that dollar. Before the advent of lotteries, racetracks were the only legalized form of gaming outside of Atlantic City. The lotteries started hitting the ground hard in the '80s, and that changed everything, which coincidentally was also during the peak time of brand-new racetracks being built and existing places revamping. The competition dynamic changed tremendously once the customer had other options. Then slot machines came to the racetracks, and that's one of the biggest changes in history—it drove a lot of things. You look back now and realize that when the historic FTBA pushed through the Sunday racing bill and the Minors' bill, that was a big deal. Today, families take it for granted they can take their kids to the track. So now, tracks are family entertainment in a different way.

"Old-time horsemen don't like it worth a damn," said a horseman who preferred to remain anonymous. "It's like walking into a casino. Unless you sit by the window, you can't see the track. No grandstands by the track for the people. It's a $200 million pretty building, but there is no roar of the crowd because you're inside."

Not everyone agrees with that assessment. "Everything going on these days is positive," said Don Dizney of Diamond C Farm in 2000 when stepping down as president of the FTBOA. "I'm impressed by the growth. When you can see racing on television twenty-four hours a day, and you see daily publications and websites geared to information and statistics, as well as purses escalating all over the country, the industry as a whole benefits."

"We've been through intertrack wagering, simulcasting, Sunday wagering, etc. What the tracks are doing now is their own advanced deposit wagering programs. You can go online and bet somehow. You don't have to go to a window anymore," said Dick Hancock, past executive director of the FTBA for twenty-two years (and Powell's predecessor). "The issue at stake is the size of the purses and breeders' and owners' awards, all of which are the result of percentage of a track's handle. When the public doesn't even come to the track but bets online, percentages drop."

Horsemen do their daily business in a completely different way from fifty years ago. Central Florida horsemen are as addicted to online resources as anyone else. Nearly all of the publications that used to be eagerly awaited on a weekly or monthly basis now sport their racing news daily in their e-magazines. Central Florida horsemen and women watch their horses race from the comfort of their office or easy chairs, as the race is occurring. "When I was in my twenties, we would get the *Racing Form* in the mail two days after the races were run," O'Farrell remembered." Now you get them two days before the races are run on the computer."

Everyone agrees that the proliferation and availability of information is one of the biggest changes in the industry. Said Diane Dudley:

> *We used to have the Blood Horse and the Thoroughbred Record, and we waited every week for those to come out. Unless you had direct contact with a trainer or track, it took a while to get the information, stakes and race results. Today you can get instant results, watch races all over the world, send X-rays on the internet. It's a whole new world. I can remember in the early 1970s, sitting in Bryan Howlett's living room at Tartan Farm with Scott, Jay Friedman and others, starting up the initial stages of Wire to Wire. We had no local magazines for daily information; the big magazines were monthly or weekly. So this was hugely exciting to create something where you could get the results the next day. But even then, just finding the name of a horse you bred was hard. Now you pay a dollar, go online and get the whole produce record of a horse. It really astounds me to think of the information available today.*

Over the last twenty years or so, the FTBOA has gone in a new direction to expand the market for Florida-breds since fewer tracks meant fewer horses needed. Dick Hancock remembers it well:

> *I got to be good friends with Paul Davis with the Department of Agriculture. He did trade missions and introduced me to folks who wanted to take horse breeders on trade missions. He'd get grants from Congress that covered flying, food, hotel, per diem. We went to Korea, and we developed a relationship with them. We brought them over, did seminars and it kept going. They came and spent over $2 million a year on 2-year-old sales. They have a big new track, and they love the racing. We went to China, India, Italy, Ireland a couple of times. It always worked great, but nothing like South Korea. Those trade missions brought lots of buyers back into our sales.*

Powell agreed, and the trade missions continue. In 2013, he and other breeders went to Argentina and Japan. "We believe it's part of our mandate to promote our Florida-bred industry, not just within the state or country but globally. That's where some of the great opportunities lie. Talk about some great dynamics." From about 2000 on, the international influence of Florida-breds has had a huge impact.

In May 2001, the FTBOA moved into a new facility near both the Ocala airport and the Ocala Breeders' Sales Company facilities. This brick building with brick floors has the delightful flavor of a traditional barn. Florida Equine Publications has its own wing with printing press in the back. Besides *The Florida Horse* and the daily, *Wire to Wire*, it also produces *Florida's Daily Racing Digest* and *Horse Capital Digest*, covering other breeds.

A lovely, miniature museum graces the lobby, complete with trophies and artifacts commemorating the history of an industry in which the FTBOA has played a major role. The portraits of past champions grace the long halls. A large library is open to members and visitors. As Bonnie Heath III said at groundbreaking of this building, "The FTBOA is extremely important. The efforts of this organization are what keep the dreams of Florida's breeders alive."

This building is also home to the Florida Thoroughbred Charities Inc., which has been in existence since 1990 and has raised more than $4 million for more than thirty charitable organizations within the Thoroughbred industry, including the University of Florida College of Veterinary Medicine and Animal Science Departments, 4-H and saddle clubs, the Horse Protection Association of Florida and many more. Some $300,000 is raised annually through fundraisers, including an Annual Charity/Live Auction and Stallion Season Auction.

The Florida Thoroughbred Retirement Farm, started in 2001, is another recipient of its largesse. A home for racehorses with nowhere else to go, it is located on 120 acres of past Tartan Farms. The state donated the pasture and supplies inmates as the labor. Florida is one of the few states that has not suffered criticism for equine slaughter when the campaigner can no longer earn a paycheck. Nonviolent inmates care for the horses and learn under careful guidance all the equine husbandry skills of a new career. This year-long program has resulted in new farmhands with both skill and devotion to the industry. The animal is also rehabilitated and trained for a new career. It has been a hugely successful collaboration between many entities and is praised nationwide as a humane answer to the problem of athletes that were never considered pets and now need a home.

WHEN A PASSION FOR public art stimulated two hundred painted cows in Zurich, Switzerland, in 1998 and spread the idea throughout European and American communities, the FTBOA collaborated and helped create a new organization to pursue this idea. The Thoroughbred industry had become somewhat removed from the community through the 1990s and into the 2000s. As the county exploded in population, overrunning the signature rolling green hills to set up new homes, businesses and developments, so the ratio of horse farmers to "ordinary" citizens became much less. Many in the county didn't know anything about the industry; the FTBOA thought that this would be a great way to reconnect.

While cows, pigs, turtles and even giant furniture have shown up in cities around the world, in Marion County, of course, it could only be horses. The Marion Cultural Alliance was born as a 501(c)3 with the goal of building an endowment for cultural grants. "Horse Fever" became its signature project and the FTBOA its first sponsor.

"There could not have been a more perfect match between an art project and a city," begins the *Horse Fever* booklet by Kent Weakley. "Art, inspired by the horse, gracing the streets of Ocala, 'The Horse Capital of the World.'… produced by the Marion Cultural Alliance and co-sponsored by the FTBOA. Horse Fever has united the arts community, the equine industry and the business community like no other project ever has or likely ever will. It brought tourists by the thousands while raising funds for the arts and local charities."

In 2001, before the public ever saw the first horse, the community dove into supporting the project. A horse transporter offered to transport the life-size artwork, and an emergency vehicle sponsor offered space for clear-coating the finished products. Printers offered to do the collateral, the press offered free coverage and Live Oak Plantation offered its international driving event as the time and place to put the finished products on auction, which would follow six months of being displayed around the community by sponsors. Artists were chosen to paint a herd of fifty-two horses.

Hancock remembers it well. "We had less horses and made more money than Kentucky did," he said proudly. But that's not why he recalls it so fondly. "On September 11, 2001, when the planes and the Twin Towers went down, we were sitting there on the town square with all these horses veiled and ready to break out. We didn't know what to do. We thought maybe we should cancel it. But then the mayor came to us and said, 'We need this.' We had a hole card no one knew about, and that was the American flag painted on one of the horses. I'll never forget the thousands of people on that square when we unveiled Old Glory. I still cry and get goose bumps when I think of it; it was such a moving deal."

The total proceeds of $856,000 were shared between Marion Cultural Alliance and the buyer's charity of choice. MCA started an arts endowment

Horse Fever. Photo by Charlene R. Johnson.

with the proceeds, and twenty-seven charities received awards. Charities continue to be funded through this very popular project, which unites community, arts and the Thoroughbred industry.

Some of the larger farms that had begun before the 1980s and survived would continue to do well and become the new record setters, top of the breeders' and owners' lists: Arthur Appleton's Bridlewood Farm; the Shermans' Farnsworth Farm, first under the father, Isadore, and then the son, Michael; Harry T. Mangurian's Mockingbird Farm; and John Franks's Franks Farm. Both of the latter would lead the nation's Breeder and Owner lists many years running through the 1990s and into the 2000s. New ones would come and go.

By the time Mangurian won the 1998 Breeder of the Year, he had just purchased more Tartan acres and had nearly one thousand horses. Adding to his national victory, he scored his 100th stakes winner. When his great stallion Valid Appeal retired from the breeding shed, he was the leading Florida-bred stallion of all time by earnings. Valid Appeal was one of In Reality's best sons. Andy Plattner wrote in *The Florida Horse*, "This reminds me of the 1980s when we were escalating. I think it's even better now!"

By 2003, 4,600 Thoroughbred foals had been registered in Marion County—clearly representing a recovered industry, a stronger industry. Two years later, the moment Dick Hancock heard the official results of the Horse Council and Ag census, he raced to the U.S. Patent Office to patent the title "Horse Capital of the World."™ It was painted on the side of a building in the downtown square of Ocala. The community and the Thoroughbred world celebrated together. People started touring the farms again. Assisted by movies like *Smarty Jones*, *Seabiscuit* and *Secretariat*, both local folks and tourists wanted to see the world-famous equine landscape. By 2013, the tours were staying filled all the time; one woman quit her day job to do nothing but tours.

When the second crash occurred around 2008, it was not industry-specific nor even America-specific but rather a worldwide plunge of everything we had and knew. It was a stronger, healthier industry, but due to the global nature of the crash, and the fact that real estate plummeted, carrying many businesses with it, the Thoroughbred world suffered with the rest of the world. "In the crash in the 1980s," O'Farrell remembered, "the horses all dropped in value, but we were able to say, 'Well, at least my land is still worth something.' This time, that didn't work."

Once again, a massive downswing in the production of Thoroughbreds occurred. In 2009, in an effort to assist the struggling industry, the FTBOA pushed a favorable stimulus package through the state legislature to help horse folk. Horses are exempt from sales tax when purchased from their original breeder, and breeding stock is exempt. Feed and animal health items are exempt. Certain farm equipment is either exempt or receives special treatment. Florida's greenbelt exemption provides property tax breaks for Florida horse farms. "We've maintained exemptions over the years," Hancock explained. "We aren't taxed on stallion seasons like Kentucky is. Roughly speaking, we went from a $3 million breeders' incentive package to a $15 million package. I'm proud of that. We're not the only state with exemptions, but no other state has as good a package as ours."

This time, Florida was the first to recover. The predominant 2-year-old sales did not suffer as badly as the other sales; the buyer still gets the break. According to the *Jockey Club Annual Report of Mares Bred 2012*, Florida stallions were the only ones in the top-ten Thoroughbred-breeding states or provinces in North America to produce more live foals in 2012 than in 2011. By 2012 and 2013, sales in Florida were back up, and the percentage of increased foal numbers in those years were the highest in the nation. But with fewer tracks, and a still struggling economy, few horsemen believe that the numbers will ever get back to 4,500–5,000 as in the past.

"In a way, everything is the same relatively; it's just that the pie has gotten a lot smaller," Lonny Powell explained. "Those were some real glory days for FTBA, OBS, the breeding industry. Wishing for the good old days is useless; they vanished with the computer and the lottery. I don't think we'll get to four thousand foals again; I don't even think it's necessary. The quality of what is produced is more important."

As pinhooking, agenting and boarding proliferated, and breeding became more the domain of those with a little more padding in the pockets, so this was reflected in a growth spurt of training centers and boarding facilities. Never has anyone argued that Florida is the best place in the world to raise a young horse or train over the winter. "Even California doesn't have the room that Florida has," one horseman noted. By 2013, some fifteen thousand Thoroughbreds were training in central Florida.

Like a patchwork quilt, the landscape in and around Marion County keeps evolving from big to small and smaller. The gap between the few large-farmed, wealthy owners and the hardworking masses seems to be widening, yet they all need one another. "What makes this industry work is the large, major farms of several thousand acres with a good set of stallions and top mares," Hancock said. "The rest of us have ten acres and one mare. But we couldn't be here if not for the larger farms."

O'Farrell agreed. "We're all in it together. I need the little guy with ten to twenty acres to bring his mares to breed to our stallions. We need enough horses in the sales to attract a lot of people so that I can sell my horses too. So we need the little guy as much as the big guys out here. If you don't have all those people to attract other people, nobody's making it. We're still a very important cog in the industry, so to speak, but nowadays around Marion County, it's a training center, not a breeding center. It's hard to be in the breeding business today because it costs a lot of money."

"I think it's going back to being the 'Sport of Kings,'" said Diane Dudley Parks. "But we're still here. Some people think a lot of the farms have disappeared, but we just moved a little further out. There are still a lot of people in the business, but the town has grown so much. It's a vicious cycle: it grows because of the equine industry and green spaces, then the people and businesses moving in take those green spaces over."

Bonnie Heath III agreed. "A lot more big, expensive partnerships exist these days, mostly in racing but some in breeding now. Big money gets together, and they can buy or run anything. Racing is tough; breeding is tough. If you don't love it, you really have no business in it."

"Those big farms that used to be the backbone, with all the stallions, the Mockingbirds and Tartans, they will never be replaced on the scale it used to be," said Nick deMeric. "We tend to smaller operations now for the most part. More training and more pinhooking means the industry is just different now. We have here one of the best training grounds of anywhere I've been in the world, and that's not just climate—it's backup services, facilities, expertise, labor pool and, of course, the climate."

"You know the business has changed a lot," O'Farrell said.

You've seen it. It is what it is; it's not really better than it was thirty, forty, even ten years ago. From the late '50s, when we got here, 'till today, the industry grew; it continued to expand until about ten years ago. The people have changed. The days of having the Tartan Farms or Harry Mangurians or the Philip Hofmans—they're gone. We do still have Charlotte Weber and Don Dizney, a few people like that—mainstays I would call them. But they're not as active as some of the people in the past were. If you look at it from a quality standpoint, our breeding industry was better off forty years ago than it is today. We had better stallions forty years ago on a national basis than we do today.

That's not to say it's worse. If you're young and eager and you're working at it, it's still a great business. For someone like me, it's hard to watch it change because I don't like change. When I was a kid, I lived right where the [Paddock] *mall sits. I used to ride my horse over to the Heaths' farm when there was no I-75. I could go through the field; our place joined their place. I like it the way it used to be, but that's not reality, so you deal with it. We are the largest training center in the world. There are more horses here than anywhere.*

Jay Friedman, publicity for OBS, agreed:

Now this is pinhooker heaven, training center heaven and 2-year-old sales heaven. Very few farms actually breed to sell—Ocala Stud is still the main one. Horse racing is hard. How do you compete with all the betting

La Chavelle Farm in 1984. *Photo by Jim Jernigan.*

and games available now? Casinos and lottery have taken a big cut out of our purses. Seabiscuit was the Babe Ruth in its day, but people don't get into it like that now. The generation that's in their sixties to eighties now still grew up on lots of rural farms, and horses were part of that. And we all watched westerns on TV as kids: The Lone Ranger, Gunsmoke, Roy Rogers and Flicka. We don't have anything to take that place now. The next generation is more removed from the farm and the horse. And there's a lot more competition for the betting and entertainment dollar today.

Yet those three movies—*Seabiscuit, Smarty Jones* and *Secretariat*—attracted a lot of attention. And so the competition will continue, although with fuzzier boundaries than in the "good old days." It's a smaller world. Only in Florida was a brand-new industry started and raced to the top to become a world competitor within thirty years and continue to hold its own, even lead the way still today. It is still at the top of its game, even as the game changes. Proudly, old-timers remind us that a Florida-bred still holds two records: the most championships earned in one year and the last Triple Crown.

As long as there is a human and a horse left in the world, the magic of the noble beast will still manifest. And there is still the dream of rags-to-riches. "I have a business shoeing, and the feed man has a business selling feed," said blacksmith Louie Rogers. "But one thing's for certain: we're all trying to catch lightning in a bottle."

Still, the question is asked, "What makes Florida-breds perform beyond their pedigree expectations?" As long ago as 1976, turf writer Chuck Tilley answered that question: "Maybe they don't. It may be that Florida just brings out the best that's in them."

BIBLIOGRAPHY

American Racing Manual. Daily Racing Form Press. Annual publications through 2001. New York.

Blood Horse. "The 10 Best Kentucky Derbies." 2005.

Bowen, Edward L. *Matriarchs: Great Mares of the 20ᵗʰ Century.* Lexington, KY: Eclipse Press, 1999.

The Florida Horse magazine. Ocala, FL, 1958–2013.

Haskins, Steve. *Dr. Fager.* Lexington, KY: Eclipse Press, 2000.

Johnson, Charlene R. *Florida Thoroughbred.* Gainesville: University Press of Florida, 1993.

Marion Cultural Alliance, Inc. *Horse Fever.* N.p.: Blue Sky Graphic Communication, Inc, 2001, 2002.

Rose, Elsie. *At Calder We Love You, a Horsewoman's Journal.* N.p.: apparently self-published, 1978.

―――. *Calder Loves Us; For the Thrill of It.* Bend, OR: Maverick Publications, 1985.

Siegenthaler, David A. *More of Everything Else*. N.p.: Good Times Publications, 1998.

Tilley, Chuck. Scrapbooks, mostly *Daily Racing Form* and *Morning Telegraph*, and mostly undated. Available at the FTBOA library.

Index

ABOUT THE AUTHOR

Charlene R. Johnson has been a writer all her life. She isn't sure when she started, but by the age of nine, she was writing full-length books. She still has a trunk full of these early masterpieces! Today, Charlene is a widely published writer, having been editor, staff writer, columnist and free-lancer for many years. Her work has appeared in more than thirty publications, and she had two books to her credit before this one. She has also assisted other people in the writing of five other books.

She was also horse crazy all her life, an inherent passion that had nothing to do with her family upbringing, except for the fact that she was raised in the

Photo by Ellie Hancock.

Northwest near Indian reservations, something that also imprinted her entire life with a love of the history and beliefs of the First People of America. So strong was her passion for horses that between the ages of nine and twelve, she saved her quarter allowance and babysitting money until, finally, she had $100 and bought her first horse, a cross between an Indian pony off the reservations and an ex-Thoroughbred cavalry stallion (very similar to a few mentioned in this book) brought in to help upgrade the stock on the reservations. From there, she launched straight out of college into a career with horses. She studied at the Morven Park International Equestrian Institute, where Olympic riders train, and managed several horse farms while her burgeoning writing career took hold with equestrian publications. A three-time winner of the Florida Turf Writing contest, it was the offer of a job as editor of *The Florida Horse* magazine that brought her to Florida late in 1982.

Much to her own surprise, she fell in love with the unique fragilities and strengths of the Sunshine State. After years of moving and traveling, she settled down to learn all she could about its history and its ecology. Today, her lifelong passion for the entire natural world, encompassing much more than just horses, needed to find voice, and she works on behalf of the environment in the Florida Park Service. Besides horses, she has written about everything from sailing and diving to Animal Angels. She is an active member of the national Outdoor Writers' Association and the Florida Outdoor Writers' Association.